GROWING UP
WEIRD:
REFLECTIONS ON A PATCHWORK
CHILDHOOD

a memoir by
Ann Locasio

Growing Up Weird: Reflections on a Patchwork Childhood
© Copyright 2016 by Ann Locasio

This is a work of creative nonfiction. The events are portrayed to the best of Ann Locasio's memory. While all the stories in this book are true, some names and identifying details have been changed to protect the privacy of the people involved.

Library of Congress Cataloging-in-Publication Data

Locasio, Ann
Growing Up Weird

p.   cm.

I. Memoir—self-actualization II. Family Life—Baby Boomer generation III. Travel—family life

ISBN 978-0-692-77109-9   PCN 2016952946
                           818.54 Lo   HV 1552 LO

If you look deeply into the palm of your hand, you will see your parents and all generations of your ancestors. All of them are alive in this moment. Each is present in your body. You are the continuation of each of these people.

—Thich Nhat Hanh

In the midst of winter, I found there was, within me, an invincible summer.

—Albert Camus

Live a great story.

—Ann's Coffee Mug

1

MY LIFE STARTED EARLY

"I had a family once." My friend James used to say that. Whatever I said I had, or had done, he had that or had done that once, himself.

Whenever I told him a friend was coming to visit, he would nod and rejoin, "I had a friend once."

If I told him I rose early that day, he'd say, "I got up once."

If I said I had just bathed, he'd reply, "I took a shower once." For that at least I was thankful.

Therefore, in the spirit of James, I proclaim: I had a family once.

I still do. However, they are scattered far and wide. We are not like in those long-gone days when everyone was clustered in a couple of small towns in Indiana.

I intend to share my story with you honestly…without nostalgia and without angst. This isn't a once upon a time story with a beginning, middle and end. What I have to share is a collection of observations, anecdotes, and remembrances.

I want to break the barrier of these pages and have a conversation with you—the reader—like a friend over coffee. I have had the most profound conversations over coffee. So grab a mug. Do you take cream? Sugar? My mother used to call coffee "brown, life-giving fluid." Have a cup of life… my life.

My life began with a rat in the wastebasket. Big things come from small things, maybe even from tiny things. That dead rat in my father's office trash basket, circa 1961, earned a gasp of utter disgust from my father who was working overtime one evening. He told me years later that as he sat there in his basement office, a thirty-something manager at the Gary, Indiana U.S. Steel Corporation, he glared at the gray rat, which had met his demise in the "circular file," as the waste receptacle was called.

My father cloaked himself in disappointment. He was a World War II vet who had gone to college on the GI Bill, only to end up in a dark cubbyhole of an office with gray walls and a rigor mortis rodent lying near him.

He should have been proud of the Bachelor of Science in business from Indiana University he earned, having surpassed his own father who only had a high school diploma and worked as a granite stonecutter. The roar of the machines at this job was responsible for my grandfather becoming extremely hard of hearing early in life. But my father would lament, "I did not go to college to sit in the basement of a steel company with a rat staring at me.

"I want to travel but I am not rich and do not have a trust fund." But he did have a plan, "I am going to switch jobs and get into management overseas and travel while I work. I will take my wife and two small children all over the world. It will be good for them too."

Dad's hometown was Upperville, 15 miles from Normalville. Upperville and Normalville had less to do with each other than might be assumed. There were no freeways in those days. The interstate system we take for granted was not established until Eisenhower signed the Federal Aid Highway Act of 1956. Therefore, traveling from Normalville to Upperville was a pretty big deal. Back then, my father's step-grandfather worked at the Normalville bucket factory for my great-aunt's uncle. My father's great-uncle Horace from Upperville also rented land and farmed it in Normalville. When Dad was young, he hung out with his friends at the Upperville Levee. It wasn't, as the name might suggest, near a lake, but near quarry holes, those deep pits in the ground filled with water where Indiana limestone had been extracted.

Upperville and some nearby towns have the highest quality limestone in the world. The majority of state capitol buildings as well as the Empire State Building have Indiana limestone in them. Extraction of limestone created quite a few quarry holes, which was what my young and water-loving father was mainly interested in at the time. Youngsters used to swim there (and occasionally drown) in the deep water. Dad's friend, a great swimmer nicknamed Junior Fish, drowned that way. You couldn't be too careful with quarry holes. Junior Fish dived in, hit his head on a rock, and was gone before anyone figured out what had happened.

Dad didn't talk about his family or neighbors much, but I got the impression that many of them were rather strange. For example, he told me about playing with the neighbor girl, Ilene. Ilene would come over and put ten vinyl records on the record player; then she'd leave. Dad's family enjoyed the music, but Ilene apparently didn't. What seemed to amuse my dad were the boyfriends she had named Albert Hollers, Herb Butts, and Junior Panel.

Then there were my father's two aunts, his mother's sisters—Helen and Martha—who were not only morbidly obese but also hoarders. Helen's husband Forrest, whom she called "Forrrst," watched TV with a pile of boxes on either side of him on the couch. He was as tiny and thin as Helen was tall and huge. "I always expected that the boxes would one day tumble into a pile and bury Forrrst and he'd never be seen again," my dad would say. I remember visiting them and seeing that both Helen and Martha had couches and refrigerators on their front porches. One time when I was at Martha's and had to use the bathroom, there was a clothesline where laundry had been put out to dry. It completely surrounded the commode and I had to part the clothes like curtains to get where I was going.

Helen and Martha both had their struggles, but they were very religious women and rarely laughed, (just like their Pentecostal mother, my Great Grandma McClain). The only time I saw Helen laugh was when she told us how she warned her next door neighbor, "If you smoke, the devil will get ya!" That was humor to Helen. No drinking, no smoking, and no gambling meant you had defeated Satan that day, which was good for a laugh. Helen would laugh at Satan, but not much else.

Helen did make me laugh once, which was unintentional on her part. It was on a summer day when someone had gifted her with a sheet of navy blue and red waterproof vinyl so she could make a raincoat. Helen decided she didn't need a raincoat. What she did need was a t-shirt and shorts. She used the material meant for the rain slicker to make a shirt with a zipper in the front and matching vinyl shorts. Helen was as wide as she was tall, so when she came to show off her new waterproof shirt and shorts, she made a *zheet, zheet* sound when she walked. She was so proud of her handiwork. I excused myself before I lost control.

THE UTTERLY REGULAR WORLD OF NORMALVILLE

My mother grew up in Normalville among respectable folks. The name Normalville is made up, but the town isn't. It was, and is, utterly normal. Normality has always been prized there, and everyone checks up on everyone else to be sure that they're maintaining the criteria for normalcy. A degree of eccentricity is allowed, but not to excess. The Normalville clan of Millers, and those who had married into the group, were tight knit and quirky to a degree that was within the bounds of approved normality.

The houses in those days were made mostly of wood and painted white. Some of them incorporated Indiana limestone. This was the accepted style, honored because it was so normal. Some houses had an upstairs. My grandparents' house did not. They weren't the rich folks in town. But they weren't poor either. My mother always talked like they were practically destitute, and the Great Depression hit them hard like everyone else. But my cousin told me, "They were never poor. Thomas always had the grocery store."

Thomas was my maternal grandfather. By the time I got to know him he was severely crippled, completely bald, and wore thick glasses with black plastic frames. He had been an auto mechanic in his heyday, but he was working on a car set up high on a platform, decades earlier, which collapsed on his leg. His leg was never the same again. Since it was a lot shorter than his other leg, Grandpa wore a built-up shoe, used a cane, and walked with a pronounced limp. After the accident, he could no longer repair cars so he ran the tavern on the town square. Later on he managed the grocery store my cousin referred to above.

Grandpa Miller's sister, Alice, and his other sister, Josie, were mushroom-gatherers. They had other skills too, like being fine seamstresses and cooks, but it is the morel mushrooms I remember. Those mushrooms were considered a great delicacy. Alice and Josie kept their location a closely guarded secret. Their ability to keep something under wraps would put societies such as the Masons, the Loyal Order of the Moose Lodge, the Mormons, and college fraternities and sororities to shame. Those folks wouldn't have been able to hold a candle to Alice and Josie's ability to hide something. When they died, the knowledge of where to find morel mushrooms died with them.

Recently, my cousin Cathy, Alice's granddaughter, told me that she had been there for some of those morel-gathering excursions. They happened in April in wet weather, in the woods, around tree stumps. In other words, there had to be ideal conditions for fungi, which makes sense. If someone reading this book finds morel mushrooms as a result, I have benefited humanity and my life has been worth it.

Morel mushrooms may have been exotic, but what the Normalville clan cooked and ate wasn't. I recently inherited my mother's 1955 and 1963 cookbooks from the Women's Society of Christian Service of the Normalville Methodist Church. Those bland women's recipes in 1955 didn't even have the cooks' first names on them. There was a fried chicken recipe presented by "Mrs. H.A. White" and a ham loaf by "Mrs. W.R. Carter." (Mrs. W.R. Carter was my morel-gathering Aunt Josie, who always called herself Mrs. William Carter). In 1963, most of the women began using their own first names, but not Aunt Josie. She fit in the same mold as a woman with a recipe in the dessert section. Inez Smith was one of the few who had a first name in 1955. Maybe she was a widow. But to make up for it, she had by way of apology, contributed an offering called "My Man's Cookies."

To say that the ingredients they used were bland is beyond understatement. What they cooked with might have been exotic to them, but I doubt it. In those days nobody seemed to be concerned about being exotic. However, there was a novel Italian dish called "spaghetti." If someone really wanted to go wild, they'd make it into a casserole. For a dash of adventure on the tongue, they added Worcestershire sauce to almost everything... except the desserts. Worcestershire sauce added a tangy burst of flavor. Maybe that was all the excitement they could handle. I am surprised they didn't use Worcestershire sauce in their apple pies.

I thought I was finally onto some of their more creative cooking when I ran across a hamburger fry calling for "green mangoes" only to find out that meant bell peppers. After I read those recipes, I concluded that I wouldn't dare make anything in that red plastic-ring-bound recipe book called, *Seasoned with Love*. Not only did the ingredients lack flavor by today's standards, anyone eating those dishes might die of a lard-induced heart attack.

Aunt Alice occasionally made a dish with several types of Jell-O in it. It was called "Nervous Dessert" because it shook in three colors. Alice once had a table full of dinner guests and when she presented the Nervous Dessert, she tripped. The bowl went flying. Colorful squares of Jell-O sailed into the air and landed on the table, the floor, the guests, and even the ceiling. Alice noted that it was not only the dessert that was nervous that day. Six months later, she still found colored blobs in the dining room above her head.

3

THE UNDERSIDE AND THE SHINY SIDE

Aunt Alice once said that Uncle Bill Carter and his wife, her sister Josie, the "Mrs. W.R. Carter" of the cookbooks, were some of the most racially prejudiced people on earth. Alice told me that they used the "N" word quite a bit. I had to put this in context. This was Normalville at the turn of the twentieth century. Truth is that Normalville was widely known as a headquarters for the Ku Klux Klan in the 1920s. According to an article broadcast by National Public Radio several years back, it was labeled a "sundown town" where African-Americans were expected to be gone by nightfall.

Then in the late 1960s, there was a brutal murder there. A young black woman was selling encyclopedias door to door when she was stabbed in the chest with a screwdriver. The murder went unsolved for years. "They didn't even try," my mother told me. Finally, in 2002, a woman came forward, saying she had long kept a terrible secret. She said when she was seven-years-old, she saw her father and a still unidentified man, both white, commit the crime. Her father was arrested, but died before he could face trial.

According to my mother, when one of my great-grandfathers died, a Ku Klux Klan robe and hood surfaced when survivors went through his attic. Mom said, "someone poor and ignorant probably left it there," but I disagree. I'm sure it was Grandpa's. There were plenty of Klansmen in Normalville at the time, and they all had family somewhere. And why would some hypothetical poor ignorant guest in Grandpa's house end up leaving a KKK outfit in the attic?

Questions about Normalville's level of racial tolerance still exist today. The NPR interviewer quoted a local resident saying, "When you come to Normalville, you notice it's mostly white folks." This is dead accurate according to the 2010 census, which lists the African-American population of Normalville as one-fifth of one percent. The white population is 97.5%. To be fair, groups promoting racial harmony are now at work trying to change Normalville's image. But as the NPR article was written a few years after the quoted census data, little seems to have changed and there is still work to be done.

Almost every family has fine upstanding citizens, and my family has plenty. My great-uncle was the mayor of Normalville for a while. My great-aunt ran for public office and got elected long before women did that. And almost all of them gave me lots of love. But the skeletons in the closet are what keep things interesting. I remember a man in my church quipping, "I spent a year doing my genealogy, and two years trying to keep it quiet!"

Me? I'm comfortable with ambiguity. I've got good and evil, poverty and wealth, kindness and meanness, and all the rest of it in my family. More good than bad overall. That makes me about average, I guess.

There are aspects of Normalville's heritage of which residence can be proud. It was the source of a healthful mineral water, which was discovered by accident while workers were drilling for something else important— oil or gas, most likely. Normalville soon became famous for some of the country's leading health resorts, including the Well Acres Spa. Celebrities as well as mundane folks visited the town to take advantage of the mineral water's reputed healing properties.

The town also houses a giant fish farm, alleged to be the largest mass of carp in the world. My cousin Cathy once told me that half of all those fish come from Normalville. Anyone who has a carp pond and is thinking of doing genealogy on their pet fish will probably discover that at least half of its ancestors come from Normalville, perhaps home of its great-great-grandfish.

My mother wasn't too concerned with racism, healthy water, or the fish farm back then. To her, Normalville was about visiting kinfolks and being visited by them. My cousin Cathy told me that after her mother died, she went through her old journals and was astonished to find how much visiting back and forth happened back in the 1940s and 1950s. While people kept busy just as they do today, they made time to gather in each other's houses. One journal entry stated, "At Grandma's house to eat chicken after church," another read, "We played cards at Nell's and saw the new baby last night," another was, "We all went out to Uncle Bill's farm yesterday. The kids rode the pony."

Cathy puzzled over the entries that referred to the family often gathering, "at the filling station," which was what they called gas stations. "Why would you meet at a gas station?" she wondered. Further reading led her to understand that her great-uncle, who owned the gas station, had a big enough room in it to host parties. He played a type of homemade banjo and the family would dance, far into the night, after he closed up shop. And on it went, story after story of get-togethers, casually arranged and woven into the fabric of daily life.

It seems that in America today, we are more lonely and disconnected than we have ever been. No wonder we have so many mental health issues. My maternal kinfolks were close and tight. It buffered them against the adversity of the Great Depression, World War II, illnesses, children dying young, and much more.

CONCERNING CARDS, MY FAMILY WAS ACE

I was surprised to find out how much lore there was in my family around playing cards. But it makes sense. They weren't rich, so they didn't travel when they had leisure time. Few people traveled much, or far, in those days. In fact, once my Uncle Bill Carter came back from army duty in Europe in World War II, he made a vow that he would never again leave Normalville. And he didn't. Uncle Bill left his farm only to work at the Normalville Meat Market. Everything in those days was local.

Once a person bought a few decks of cards at the local Jackson's drugstore, amusement was free from then on. In those days, Mom loved the family card game called Six-Tricks, which her Normalville family played on the back porch far into the night and on weekends. During those games the beer flowed freely and was followed by coffee to keep the card-playing senses sharp. She loved her parents' white wooden house with ten steps in front that led to a substantial front porch with green wicker rocking chairs. When she married my father, she assumed she would stay relatively close to the family, the Six-Tricks games, and the beer. And she assumed she would always be able to rock in the green wicker rocking chairs when she came to visit in the summer.

My father found the clan tough to marry into, but they accepted him at last, even him being "Italian and all" because he learned to play Six-Tricks. Whenever the family needed a person to make the required foursome, Dad was right there. I learned from him that playing other people's favorite games is a great way to make friends.

The card playing occasionally got emotional. Uncle Harvey, Grandma Miller's oldest brother, played the game with a ferocious intensity. He was normally a genial salesman (he was the town's Buick dealer). He was a huge man both horizontally and vertically. The family had their usual two card tables, one in the kitchen and the other on the back porch. The back porch was not large; the card table took up most of the space there. The gathering that night was bigger than usual, so the kinfolks were playing "raise." This meant that the losing team had to vacate their spots, or "raise" themselves up and out of their chairs, so that two other people could replace them and play the winners.

Uncle Harvey entered the back porch to take the place of one of the losers. He struggled to get his corpulent frame into the narrow space between the chair, table, and wall. On the first go-round, one of his opponents, my Aunt Maggie, got a fabulous hand and "shot the moon." This meant that she made a bet that she could win all the points. She succeeded. Poor Uncle Harvey had to immediately haul his massive frame out of the space and retreat. It was one of the few times this mild-mannered salesman ever swore.

The family had all kinds of card-related slang. If you made spades trumps, the superstition said that, "they're in the widow," meaning if you were the bidder, you'd always find spades in the leftover pile of cards you got to pick up and use. It didn't seem to happen any more often than the odds would predict, but the saying persisted.

"Widow" is a sexist term, I know, but that's what they called it. "Widow" was sometimes called "the Widdee" by my Grandpa Miller, who tended to invent creative pronunciations for all kinds of words. For example, he called waffles "WA-ffles" with a short A like in 'cat'. The other nicknames for clubs, diamonds, and hearts respectively, were Black Faced Clubbolius, Red Faced Dia-Made, and Hearty-Man Ate a Toad-Frog.

Grandpa Locasio, who learned to play Six-Tricks as skillfully as he played poker, called a Queen a "Mop-Squeezer."

If Grandma Miller picked up a terrible hand, she would lament, "I got a dog from every town."

Cards were both social life and socialization. Over a card table, one learned to take acceptable risks, manage emotion, win and lose gracefully. Or not. If the score was close, an uncle or aunt would observe, "The folks are as good as the people." If someone got too involved in talking, someone would cut in, "Shut up and deal." One learned teamwork by playing with a partner, to figure out how to win together and enjoy the shared triumph. Sometimes partners lost together and if one's bidding was at fault, one had to be appropriately contrite.

I learned early that "the winners laugh and tell jokes, and the losers say, 'Deal!'" My father got schooled, early in his marriage to my mother, on the necessity of dealing the cards quickly when it was his turn. Once, later in life, we were all playing cards and we noticed that Dad would pick up the cards and pass them out whether it was his turn or not. My partner at the time patted Dad on the shoulder. "We're going to have to send Dad to Gambler's Anonymous. He's a compulsive dealer!"

My family prided itself on being smart. In the decade before the World War II GI Bill, few of them went to college because they could not afford it. But they had a flair for business and did well with the stores, dealerships, and restaurants they ran. My mother inherited her family's business acumen. These smart, sharp people had little patience with the slow-witted or those who had poor judgment, such as my grandmother's neighbor Ethel who had a string of unemployed boyfriends after her husband Pete was killed in a car accident. Once Pete died, Ethel, probably overcome with grief, let her kids run wild.

The family took a dim view of Ethel and those of her ilk and would mutter, "Ever since Pete died, Ethel doesn't know shit from Shinola."

One might get the impression, looking at the serious photos of my family that are typical of people in the 1940s, that my forebears were polite and decorous people. Well...some were and some weren't. Aunt Catherine, who married Great-Uncle Harvey, was the epitome of respectability.

She had dark hair and eyes and delicate features. She could have been a Southern belle from Louisiana. She even talked with a Southern accent. The devout Catholic would have been perfect, sitting on an antebellum mansion porch, waving a lacy cardboard fan and sipping a mint julep.

In contrast, Great-Aunt Josie, Great-Aunt Alice, and Cousin Helen Carter, daughter to Uncle Bill Carter, were my foremothers in irreverent behavior. They frequently gathered to gossip, drink beer, smoke cigarettes, tell jokes, and swear like sailors. Helen Carter once declared, "One day I'm going to die suddenly in my sleep, go to heaven, and surprise the shit out of everyone."

5

HOOSIERISMS

My parents' families spoke in Hoosierisms. Hoosierisms were the expressions used by these small town residents of Indiana the "Hoosier State."

The following is a compilation of these figures of speech. They wouldn't all be used in one conversation, but this one is constructed out of all the Hoosierisms I "ever heard tell of" and that my cousin Cathy has written down and stored up.

Imagine a long dining table full of relatives and a china cabinet behind them full of floral plates and cups. Off to the side there's a dark wooden end table with a black rotary dial phone and address book on it, along with a black plastic container of pens for writing messages. Empty casserole dishes and salad bowls litter the table along with half-empty water, wine, and beer glasses. Blue and white striped coffee mugs dot the scene. Knives, forks, and crumpled up yellow cloth napkins lay on the used white ceramic dinner plates.

"Josie, with those dresses you made my little granddaughters, you outdid yourself."

"Well Mary, I just about wore myself out, but they're done now. For a while I was sewing to beat the band. I'm just plumb tuckered out. I thought I wouldn't get them done in time for Ann Lee's birthday. I was worried to death about it."

"Ann Lee looks as cute as a button wearing that dress. Now I'm going to get my tomatoes set out. And I'm going to pick my last mess of beans."

(Uncle Howard cuts in)

"I spent all last night fixing the car. When it was done I just about keeled over."

"That new Buick you got is a dandy. Now that it's fixed, you can rest on your laurels."

"I.U. will play Purdue right off the bat this season. I hope Purdue gets out there and dribbles fancy. Right out of bounds."

"Smarty pants."

"Sure was glad to meet Mark's fiancée, Nancy, last week. We think an awful lot of her. She was wearing one of those pencil skirts when I saw her last. That was some getup."

"Whoo-ee."

"I heard tell that the Normalville Fall Festival will be bigger than the whole town square can hold this year."

"It can't get that big. I never heard tell of such a thing."

"Lots more clubs and churches are getting in on the act. The Elks Club is having a booth there for the first time. I put up ten quarts of pickles to sell there. And Debbie Hart is a sure thing for Festival Queen this year. She's mighty purty. And she's not stuck up about it."

"Glad to hear it. Last year's queen was a little too big for her britches. Miss High and Mighty."

"She was a doozie."

"Well, my stars."

"She sure was a sight."

"Criminy! What's that racket? Good Gosh a'mighty, what the Sam Hell is that?"

"It's the kids playing tag. Billy! Cut that out! If you run through the dining room one more time, I'm gonna slap you to sleep. You just set down there and clean up your plate."

"How's Joe doing at the lumber yard?"

"Quit after a week. It's about time he got him a job o'work. I saw him outside Thomas's tavern last night, drunk as a skunk. I've never seen one like him in all my born days. And I'll tell you right now, he's the meanest cuss that ever was."

"Did I ever tell you that Lillian told me two months ago that I didn't know how to raise kids? I wanted to slap her silly. I'll tell you right now, I said to her, I raised my kids right. And she's had more than enough trouble with hers. 'Don't start preaching to me about raising kids,' I told her. 'What's your excuse? You're a one to talk. You'd better watch your p's and q's.' She got her nose out of joint about it, but that's just plain ornery."

"Well, my sakes alive!"

"And that Lillian's got a hind end as big as a porch."

You could probably tell from that last comment that the family never did like Aunt Lillian. I never was sure why. Uncle Howard called her "the fiddle woman" because he said she had a figure like one.

Aunt Lillian married into the family like my dad, but wasn't successful in being accepted. It was probably because she had no sense of humor, didn't tell dirty jokes, and refused to play Six-Tricks. My father learned from her misery and used it to shape his strategy for social acceptance. It wasn't easy for him either, but over time he became one of the gang. Still, Aunt Lillian had the last laugh. She outlived them all, passing away in a nursing home at the age of 92. Sometimes you don't have to defeat them. You just have to outlast them.

Anyway, my mother grew up hearing all kinds of Hoosier talk. I guess if you're surrounded by Hoosierisms all your life, you could get homesick for them. Mom did.

6

YANKEE TRANSPLANTS, RE∘PLANTED

The Hoosierisms, and the Six-Tricks games, beer, and coffee were about to end for many years starting in 1961. My mother was heartbroken over the news. She had to leave her nearby close family in Normalville. Unlike my restless father who couldn't wait to get away from his kinfolks, she had no desire to leave the close-knit network of support she enjoyed just a couple of hours away from where she and my father lived in Hobart, near my father's job in Gary. I have no recollection of the marital fights and tears over my father's job change to a company called Booz Allen & Hamilton, where he would assume the title of Management Consultant. His work had him as an efficiency expert in cost accounting at the steel company, using an accounting system called Standard Cost. When he tried to explain it to me years later my eyes would glaze over. Accounting simply was not my *amour propre*.

My father did not love it either. What he loved was having someone else do all the figuring and summarizing, so he could tell the world about it. My father delighted in making presentations with flair in front of large audiences with his Italian arms gesticulating wildly. So while he did not love accounting, he loved talking about it to anyone who would listen. For that matter, my father would talk about anything to anyone who would listen.

My mother was fine with my father's title and jobs and presentations. What horrified her was that the steel company for which my father was going to work on behalf of Booz Allen & Hamilton was in the British Isles, in Wales. My mother was expected to fill the role of housewife and entertainer *extraordinaire* for the clients at Spencer Works Steel, located in Cardiff in what is now the country called *Cymru*. She and my father would be flying overseas to take up residence in the town of Newport, Monmouthshire (now Newport, Gwent) with two little children, my younger sister and me, aged eight months and almost two years, respectively. My sister flew in a crib on the wall of the airplane and cried most of the way. Perhaps my mother felt the same way she did.

My father, however, was as excited as a little boy at Christmas. The dead rat that had stared at him from the wastebasket was soon to be a distant memory. He was thrilled to be headed overseas. This being the early 1960s, my mother had no say in the long-distance move. She was just a housewife. Such were the times they lived in and for a middle class family with a solo breadwinner husband, she was expected to follow along and support him. She did. But not without major resentment. She talked often about missing home and wanting to go back and sit at her parents' white kitchen table atop the blue linoleum floor, playing Six-Tricks and drinking beer followed by coffee.

My father assured her that this was merely a temporary assignment, two to three years at the most, so she kept her chin up and comforted herself with the thought that before long, she would be back home. If she had known about Booz Allen & Hamilton and the additional assignments my father cooked up with them, which included not returning to the USA for twelve years, she would have been less sanguine.

My half-Italian father charmed everyone he met. He looked completely Italian with his slicked-back dark hair, Roman nose, and squat build. He was positively glamorous in his business suits when he went to work, in crisp white shirt, striped silk tie, silver tie pin, cuff links, black jacket, neatly pressed black slacks, wing tip shoes, and the prosperous smell of the cigars he smoked. His consolation prize, as it were, to my mother was that because he was making a much bigger salary in Wales than he had been in Gary, Indiana, she could hire a nanny to take care of my sister Lisa and me. That would free up lots of her time to go sightseeing with friends and colleagues they would meet.

They did meet others and would visit all over Wales, England, and Scotland when Dad was not working. They got Abergavenny, the St. Pierre Country Club and Hotel, Swansea, Bristol, Loch Ness in Scotland. I got a nanny, a chest full of toys, a giant bedroom with a fireplace, a doll named Josephine, and later, a Welsh nursery school.

I have no memory of flying across the Atlantic. I am sure there were tearful farewells all around between my mother and her entire Normalville family. My mother lost her proximity to her best friend, Gloria Nelson, as well. Gloria lived next door to my mother in her home near Gary, Indiana. Mom would lose her ability to slip next door to hang out with Gloria when the housecleaning and laundry were caught up. My mother had no idea if they would ever again share an entire can of Hershey's cocoa powder in a single morning, accompanied with giggles. Mom and Aunt Gloria Nelson shared the same passion for chocolate that I had for years. They would no longer be able to get together to complain about their husbands, since both my father and Uncle Lewis were difficult men to be married to.

While Lewis and my father eventually became best friends, my father's first impression of Uncle Lewis at U.S. Steel was that he was "a grouch." There was truth to it. The balding, tall, thin Lewis had a heart of gold, but he turned grumbling into an art form.

Lewis had plenty of opportunities to practice grumbling. His favorite battleground was ordering breakfast in restaurants. In the early 1960s it was virtually impossible to order oatmeal accompanied by brown sugar. Uncle Lewis took it as a challenge. He loved brown sugar on oatmeal and equally he loved to fight for it. Aunt Gloria sat through many a cantankerous conversation between Lewis and the wait staff at restaurants as Lewis energetically advocated for having brown sugar as an oatmeal menu option. Then came the day we were all driving back from a family trip after spending a weekend at Burr Oak State Park in Ohio. We left early in the morning and stopped at a local restaurant for breakfast. Dad looked at the menu and showed it to Lewis. "Look, buddy! Oatmeal with brown sugar!"

Gloria started laughing. "Lewis won't order that. It's too easy!"

One day, my father found out that Lewis loved cribbage as much as he did. When he found out Lewis played, it was the beginning of 50 years of being best buddies. Lewis grumbled all the way through many a cribbage game, especially when he was losing. But even when he was winning, he grumbled because he wasn't winning by high enough margins. He and my father kept score with pegs on Dad's wooden cribbage board. They played for high stakes. It cost a penny a point and a quarter a game for the loser. At the end of several games, Lewis might owe Dad seventy-three cents. He always paid up, but grumbled the whole time.

Those two accountants kept score meticulously and always exactly settled the balance after every session. I have an iconic photograph on my bookshelf of Dad and Lewis at Burr Oak State Park playing cribbage. They had forgotten to bring a cribbage board, but they were accountants after all. They kept score with columns of figures on sheets of paper. The next morning when we all got up, we discovered those two guys had played until 3:00 a.m. The stack of papers was six inches high.

Lewis had a side business doing people's income taxes. This suited him admirably because he could fight there too. His second-favorite indoor sport, after contending with breakfast wait staff, was going to an audit on behalf of dear little old ladies who had been audited by the IRS. (Those are the same people my little brother, Hankley, once referred to as the Eternal Revenue Service).

Tax professionals quailed in their shoes when they saw Lewis coming. He would prepare for hours and enter the auditor's office like a gladiator in a Roman arena. His preparation and knowledge of tax law were wielded like verbal swords. He rarely lost in combat. After the parrying and thrusting, he headed home to a grateful old lady and then a restaurant, to fight for a bowl of oatmeal and brown sugar.

I wonder if Dad missed Lewis. Perhaps he did, but he was so carried away with working overseas and loving it, I never heard him say he missed his friend. All these years later, I wonder if part of the reason Dad drank so much was that lost connection. Dad was a man of many secrets, I was later to find out, and that may have been one of them. I also wonder if much of what drove Dad overseas was a desire to get away from his entire family. My mother had a large network of close kinfolks, but Dad couldn't get away from his family fast enough.

Dad had reasons for plotting his escape. He had his Italian Grandma Miletti who shrieked and smelled of garlic. There was Grandma McClain who was Pentecostal, was not allowed to cut her hair, wore long skirts and plain black shoes, and would not allow card playing on Sundays. Her brother was the severely alcoholic Uncle Glenn.

Dad's own father, my Grandpa Locasio, was a gambling addict in those days. His own mother was depressed and cleaned the house compulsively. And his younger sister, Rose, was jealous of him for being a boy, being older, and having far more privileges. When Dad got home from dates and tried to sneak in after curfew in the dark, he found that Rose had rearranged the living room furniture so he would trip over it.

So my father was happy to flee, while my mother was torn from her roots, as they boarded the plane for Wales.

INTO THE DANK WET COLD...PLUS COAL

I t could not have been easy for my mother to fly with two small girls, aged two and eight months. Changing diapers on the plane must have been challenging. Sitting on the long flight, dreading what was to come, and having to find her way around in a foreign country must have been overwhelming. Although it was summer when they flew to Europe, Wales was cold and wet when they arrived. They stayed in a hotel while they waited for their shipment of furniture to arrive from across the Atlantic. My mother told me later about ordering some soup for my sister, and what arrived was a lumpy beef broth with a layer of grease on top.

Fortunately, they soon met a nurse named Anne Bodann in a doctor's office when one of us got sick. She took the young couple under her wing and helped my parents with the culture shock. Anne was pivotal in my life. She helped my mother, and she also gave her the name of an agency that had nannies for hire. Thus Anne was responsible for the nanny who burst into my consciousness as soon as I was old enough to remember anything.

The nanny's name was Brenda Jones. At least, that is her name now. (Names in this story have been changed to protect both the guilty and the innocent, and Brenda was one of the guilty). She is part of many of my earliest memories, and I still remember her slaps. She was a good actor, in that she acted the part of a young woman who loved children. The reality

23

was that for the slightest misstep—and at age three, I made many of them—she would hit my sister and me. I had many a red, sore rear end in those days. She told us we must never tell our mother or father that she had hit us. Of course we never did. We feared what else she might do to us if we told.

She once put my sister in a playground swing designed for older children. My sister fell out of the swing and cried in pain. Brenda again extracted a vow of silence from both of us and warned us of consequences too dreadful to mention if we ever leaked news of this incident to anyone else. I found out later, to my surprise, that there was an eyewitness to this incident. Our elderly neighbor, Eleanor Jones, saw it happen from her top floor apartment. She told my parents about it after Brenda had left their employ. My parents demanded, "Why didn't you tell us at the time?" Eleanor shrugged. "I didn't want to interfere."

My very earliest memory is of Brenda with a furious face, brown disheveled hair, eyes wide and mouth clamped shut, ready to spank me. Because I was so small, she looked enormous. In my mind's eye, when I looked up, it was as if I was looking up at a tall building. I can still recall seeing the whites of her eyes when she was in a fury. When the whites appeared, a slap would follow. Later, the poster of a maniacal Jack Nicholson in the movie *The Shining* reminded me of Brenda in a white-hot temper.

She came from a poor family. Jobs in Wales, especially for young women, were scarce. I doubt that Brenda would have chosen to be a nanny if she had had any other options. Brenda herself had been raised the way she was raising us. Her mother had been the head of a school for nannies where she trained students on how to give young children a strict upbringing to build character. Corporal punishment was integral to the curriculum.

About eight years later, when my youngest brother was a year old, I hit Hankley when he grabbed my long hair and yanked it.

"No slapping," my mother told me.

Unlike us, Hankley was never spanked or hit. Except by us when nobody was looking. It was only fair, we reasoned.

8

EXISTING, WHILE TIME PASSED

Brenda had an inflexible rule. We were never to disturb her in the morning. If we did, we would hear, "You'll get a smack after breakfast." On those days, cereal could taste like sawdust and eggs stuck and coagulated in my dry mouth. Most days, I could not remember talking loudly or remember what I did that woke Brenda. No matter. If she had been awakened by us, we would inevitably hear at the end of breakfast, "Let's go and have a smack."

An odd remnant from those days lingers. When someone says, "Let's go have a snack," I initially hear the word "smack" and my heart stops for a minute.

Brenda's slaps would elicit screaming and crying, which only caused Brenda to promise to smack us again if we didn't stop. Then she would say, "You're going to go outside, and you're going to stay outside. Don't you dare knock on the door to come in the house. I'm going to lock the back door. When it's time to come in, I'll unlock it."

Once she did call us back in, Brenda would then take us for our daily walk down the high street. My sister rode in the stroller while I marched faster than I thought possible to match Brenda's stride so she would not leave me behind. If I didn't keep up, that would be the consequence and she would warn, "You'd deserve it." If I asked her to slow down, she would say, "N-O spells NO!"

If I asked to ride in the stroller for a change, I was told, "Stand and walk on your own two feet." Brenda believed in self-sufficiency for three-year-olds. At lunch, we drank our milk out of red or yellow plastic cups. When I asked Brenda if I could have a red cup instead of a yellow one, she would declare, "You'll have what you're given." Then she would purposefully give me a yellow one. I learned from Brenda not to ask for things lest I be punished for it. I lived that way for a long time. Asking for anything could be dangerous. It was a revelation to me years later that others asked for what they wanted and often got it.

My other memory of Brenda is of eating tomato soup on a cold Welsh winter day, a day so cold that a glass of water froze overnight after being left over from a party in the lounge. In the kitchen, warmed by the stove, Brenda broke white bread into bite-sized pieces and crumbled it in our soup. We ate soggy, soup-soaked bread. My mother later told us she thought that bread in soup was disgusting, but she never said anything at the time to Brenda or to us.

Most days on the mandatory walk, Brenda hustled me down the high street and through ten black posts that divided the sidewalk on the main street from the walkway to the park. Those posts were about three feet tall and arranged in a triangular pattern like pool balls before the cue stick breaks them. They smelled like coal smoke. I wondered if the posts had started out brown or green, or even white, and turned black from the soot in the air. Something mysterious beckons me to go see those black posts again, if they still stand. I am sure they will look smaller (they were a head shorter than I was at age four). Seeing those posts again would be like a soldier returning to a now peaceful battlefield to acknowledge one's survival. Tredegar Park, where Brenda took us, still exists. I discovered that online. But the old wooden seesaws, tall slide, steel climbing frame, and metal merry-go-round are long gone, replaced by a play scape.

I had my first experience at a concession stand during the summer of 1963 at the park. I was sent to buy a British fizzy lemonade for Brenda, but could not figure out the process of asking for one, then paying for it.

I found that difficult at age three, but Brenda was angry that I could not manage it and there were tears.

I can see in my mind's eye being at the lunch table with my sister and my mother eating a pot roast. I got a piece of meat that was full of gristle. I chewed and chewed but could not swallow it. Brenda smiled at my mother. "I'll take her to the bathroom and help her get rid of it." She led me away from the table into the bathroom. When we were alone, I saw the whites of her eyes and her pursed lips. "Swallow it."

"I can't."

"I *said* swallow it."

I chewed and chewed. Somehow I got it down. We returned to the table. "Poor Ann. I'm glad I was able to help her," Brenda smiled sympathetically at my mother, who smiled back at her.

Later, our neighbor, Eleanor Jones (every other person in Wales was named Jones, at least in those days) at the apartment complex, told my mother and father that she had been troubled by the way Brenda had treated Lisa and me. She told them this long after Brenda had left our employ.

Again my parents asked, "Why didn't you say something before now?"

Again Eleanor replied, "I didn't want to interfere."

When my mother recounted what Eleanor had said, I asked her, "If you saw Brenda today, what would you say to her?" I waited to hear how my mother would have confronted Brenda for what she had done. My mother shrugged. "I'd tell her hello."

The day Brenda left, she came into our bedroom and kissed Lisa and me goodbye for the last time. She said some affectionate words in my mother's presence, and Mom nodded approvingly. I felt a stab of uncontrollable joy as I watched Brenda turn away.

I can still recall her light blue raincoat and patterned silk head scarf disappearing through the doorway, and the shiny white purse on her arm. As that figure receded out the door, it was as if tight iron bands around my waist had been suddenly cut and I was free to move for the first time.

Brenda left us early in 1964. The reason I know this is by The Beatles songs that were playing on the radio. Brenda loved The Beatles and used to hum their tunes when she was in a good mood. A sense of vigilance kicks in when I play "Please, Please Me," "All My Loving," "She Loves You Yeah Yeah Yeah" and "I Want to Hold Your Hand." When I move on to "A Hard Day's Night," which was released in 1964, I no longer feel tightness in my body.

We saw Brenda one more time in Wales when we encountered her in the Newport high street. My mother and she exchanged greetings. I said nothing. And then she was gone forever, except in memory.

Those memories linger. Even today I startle easily. When someone yells, waves an arm near my face, or shows the whites of their eyes in anger, I remember Brenda's hand coming into my peripheral vision, swooping down to hit me.

9

CRASS UNCLE CLAYTON

Once Brenda left, I could more easily appreciate the beauty of Wales. The view of the Pennine Mountain range seen from our living room window was lovely in its curvaceous heights. Purple heather covered the mountains like a soft shag carpet. The weather, however, was not quite so lovely. The weather forecast in Newport was always the same, "Cold, with rain coming over the Pennines." My father joked that that wasn't a real weather forecaster on TV; they just had a puppet mouthing the words and played the same tape over and over. Even with the cruddy weather, Wales was and is a beautiful country.

And then there was Clayton Berry. "Uncle Clayton" was not my real uncle, nor was his wife, "Auntie Armal," my real aunt. I had so many people I called "uncle" and "aunt" in those days, that for a long time I was unsure about who my biological extended family really was. Clayton and Armal showed up in Newport, Wales; in Dortmund and Dusseldorf, Germany; and later in London. Everywhere we lived, the Berrys would appear. At the time, I had no inkling of how unusual this was. The family would move, and then like clockwork, the Berrys would be knocking on the door again. The way it worked was like this: Dad would start a consulting job in the cost accounting role, but before long, he would require the services of an engineer who understood the intricacies of the steelmaking process. Enter Clayton Berry.

Clayton was over six feet tall, with large hands and feet. He was strong enough to hold Lisa and me in each of his arms at the same time when we were four and five years old. He never had much hair. Initially it was light brown and barely covered his head. Later, he went mostly bald and wore glasses. He had the most wonderful buck-teeth that stuck way out when he smiled. Dad and Clayton didn't always get along well, but they were stellar coworkers. Being coworkers in those days required a certain amount of cocktail-party socializing with colleagues and their wives—and it was always wives, not husbands, back then.

Mom wasn't that fond of Armal, but she tolerated her. I liked the Berrys. They were the stereotypical fat and jolly couple who could and did eat massively. And they ate well because they could afford it on Clayton's salary. Clayton could get away with it somewhat, because of his size. His feet were twelve inches long; I know that because as an assignment for school I measured them and found that his foot measured exactly one foot in length. That was important at the time because I had to tell the whole first-grade class about it, so I remembered.

Armal, was short and was as wide as she was tall because there was little room for the excess adipose to go. I do not exaggerate. She may have been even wider than she was tall. She had black wavy permed hair, which later went grey. She had triple chins, wide jowly cheeks, and extra rolls of fat on her neck. Her body looked like vertical ocean waves rippling down.

One time, we went over to the Berrys's lavish home for "English tea." Armal was an excellent cook. She put on a spread of homemade pizza, the first and last time I ever had pizza for tea. During the hearty repast, which included not only pizza and tea, but a sizable pile of scones, crumpets, and clotted cream, Armal said to her teenage daughter Cathy, "Be sure and eat plenty, honey. We won't be eating again until after we see the movie tonight and have that four-course dinner at the Connaught Hotel."

My mother often used the Berrys as a negative example of greed and gluttony, but it didn't seem to hurt them any. And the food we shared with them over the years was gourmet and satisfying. The meals were joyously fun because Clayton had not only an outlandish appetite, but also an outlandish sense of humor. According to my father, who saw that side of him where I did not, Clayton could be gauche. He sometimes said, "It's a good thing we're not all alike, otherwise everyone would want my wife."

Dad would roll his eyes. He'd later snort to my mother, "Can you imagine a bunch of guys fighting over Armal?"

But the Berrys loved each other and were married over 40 years.

Clayton played all kinds of games with us, which was one reason I always looked forward to the Berrys coming over. He taught us to play Buzz-Bang where we took turns counting from one to a hundred. For multiples of six, instead of saying the actual number, we said, "Bang." For multiples of seven, we said, "Buzz." The clever engineer had found a fun way for us to learn math.

Armal taught us, "Pease Porridge Hot, Pease Porridge Cold, Pease Porridge in the Pot, Nine Days Old!" with accompanying hand clapping motions. After they left, Lisa and I played it for months.

I learned from my father that at cocktail parties, and also sometimes in the office, Clayton showed his gauche side. When the weather turned chilly he would wander into my father's office and say, "It's as cold as a well-digger's ass in the Klondike." During a hard rain, he announced to my father, "That sounds like a cow pissin' off a two-hundred foot cliff onto a flat rock." While he would be crassly coarse in front of the guys, Clayton tried never to show it in front of the "ladies." But occasionally he slipped.

He was traveling with my father and his mother, my Grandma Locasio, when Grandma was visiting in Europe. The adults all went on a vacation to France. For the first time, all of the travelers encountered a bidet. For the uninitiated, it is something to sit on after using the restroom, which gently sprays water upward to clean off any residue. After Clayton finished with the bidet, he walked out of the restroom and exclaimed to my father, "Goddam it, Vic, that's the fanciest ball-washer I've ever seen!"

In the next moment he was standing face to face with Grandma, who heard the whole thing. Grandma gaped. Clayton turned purple.

10

TULIPS, WOODEN SHOES, AND WINDMILLS

We traveled with the whole Berry family to Holland on vacation in 1966. I know it was 1966 because I remember The Beatles' new song "Ticket to Ride" was playing on the German radio just before the trip. The Germans liked The Beatles too; they had them before the British did. The Beatles spent a few years playing in Hamburg before exploding onto the British music scene.

My parents had the less than joyous experience of five continuous days with the Berrys. Working with Clayton was tolerable, cocktail parties with Armal were acceptable, but five days of coexistence strained the social fabric pretty hard.

Unaware of this, I had the joyous experience of seeing Holland. It was flat. The only land that is flatter than Holland is Amarillo, Texas. But Holland was a lot prettier. Everywhere I saw vividly colored red, pink, and yellow tulips. What I wanted to see was wooden shoes. I already had a Dutch doll at home wearing them, and I pleaded to be taken somewhere to see real people who had them on. Armal found a street market where vendors wore old-fashioned Dutch costumes, including wooden shoes. I was thrilled.

Mom said later, "You shouldn't have bothered Armal that way about wooden shoes! She wasted all that time looking for them!" But I was thrilled.

Also thrilling were all those huge windmills. They were used in centuries past to drain the low-lying country's lakes, wetlands, and swamps after dams were built. In the sixteenth century people modified the structure of windmills, and they were then used to produce oil and paper and to saw timber. During our vacation, I noticed how they seemed to be everywhere and wished we could take one home and put it in the yard.

The highlight of the trip was our visit to Madurodam, the town that has a model village in it that is an exact replica of the town itself. The Dutch houses were my height. The church steeple was slightly taller. The village was combed with tiny railroad tracks with working trains running on them. The trains went in and out of tiny tunnels and somehow never collided with each other. The airport had planes taxiing all over the place. For the rest of my life, I have loved miniature everything. Ideally, I would like to transplant Madurodam to my Texas home. My backyard would be an ideal place for it. Right next to the windmill.

Many years later, Dad retired and no longer went to his office or worked with Clayton. In retirement he wrote to Ripley's Believe It Or Not to tell them how he and Clayton had worked together all those years. Ripley's was intrigued enough to follow up on it, and asked Dad to send photos of himself and Clayton. The cartoon of the two men actually ran as a Ripley's column in all the daily newspapers one day in the 1980s. Both Dad and Clayton got a framed copy from Ripley's. It said, "V.J. Locasio and C.H. Berry have worked together for over 30 years…BUT IN 4 COMPANIES, 12 COUNTRIES AND ON 3 CONTINENTS!"

And they never even liked each other all that much.

11

TRAINS AND TRAUMA

When I think of all the things that
would have never been if you had never
been, I celebrate the day you were born.
—Dan Fogelberg

Because if you had never been, you wouldn't be here listening to my stories. And I do love an audience.

Most of the time when we lived in Europe was pretty routine. We weren't on vacation all that much. I wish we had been. I want to live a life where I'm on vacation 351 days a year and only work two weeks. I got the math right, didn't I? Because 351 plus 14 equals 365, right? I don't want to be like my friend Allie who says, "Sixty percent of the time I'm good at math, the other seventy percent of the time I'm not."

I digress. But life is context and my current outlook is influenced by my experience, even one from fifty years ago.

I loved watching the trains in Newport and visiting the railroad station. The mystery of trains appearing from unknown places, people getting on and off, and then disappearing riveted my attention. It seemed magical. I fantasized about walking along those tracks for many miles to see where they led. I might possibly end up in a magical utopia. I eventually learned that I could only end up in places much more prosaic.

Instead of a magical utopia, I got the city of Cardiff, which actually wasn't bad. I once took the train to Cardiff with my mother on a nursery school holiday. The dining car, where we bought orangeades to drink while the scenery passed by, was a thrilling adventure. In those days, every experience was new. Even the labels on the orangeade bottles bought in the dining car were worthy of examination. (The brand was Kia-Ora, an orange-colored, sugary liquid of zero nutritional value and infinite pleasure-inducing ability). The rattle and click of the wheels, the cows and sheep passing by in the green fields outside, and afternoon tea later at the Queen's Hotel, remain an indelible memory. It was the first time I had seen white linen tablecloths and napkins. That made a deep impression.

I also enjoyed the bread sticks and the silver toast racks that held paper-thin slices of very dark brown crispy, curvy slices of toast, which snapped apart under the slightest pressure. They were delicious with the marmalade my mother spread on them. The women having tea at the Queen's Hotel had on dark dresses and stiletto high heels, just like my mother did. I wondered how they all walked so many miles in such uncomfortable shoes.

At the apartment, Lisa and I played dress-up in my mother's clothes. That is how I learned exactly how difficult those high-heeled shoes were to wear. We called ourselves, for unknown reasons, Mrs. Alp and Mrs. Will. What fun it was to pretend to be grown up like my glamorous mother, with her raincoat draped over me and trailing behind as I walked with gold earrings clipped to my ears as I teetered on the stiletto heels.

I was disappointed when our games had to cease when I caught the measles. I was more disappointed when I got better, expecting to resume the role of Mrs. Alp. But nothing is more contagious than measles, so Lisa came down with them too. My anxious parents kept the lights low, as one of the complications of measles was blindness, or so it was believed at the time. Not realizing this, I found the constant dim lights annoying.

Lisa, after she got over the measles, had another crisis. It began innocently enough, with the two of us playing rough and tumble games on our bunk beds. Like a snapshot, I recall her raising up on the top bunk, laughing over a joke I had told, right before she plunged off the bed head-first, landing with her skull banging on the hard stone floor below. There was screaming as I ran to my parents. "Lisa fell out of the bunk bed!"

To this day, I can see my small sister laughing, her expression turning from joy to surprise and fear as she tumbled over the side of the bed. Stop. Freeze frame. In the next moment, dead silence. Then screaming. The screaming went on and on.

The next event I remember was the trip to the hospital. Lisa was kept overnight for observation. In those days, parents were not allowed to stay, so we all came home. I wonder what that was like for Lisa. All she told us the next day was "I ate jelly," which was what the Welsh called Jell-O. But did she call out for her mother in the night? What was it like for that three-year-old to be left alone in a huge hospital with strange doctors and nurses? What tests did they run for concussion? Did anyone try to explain to her what was going on?

When we picked her up the next day, she was fine except for a monstrous black eye that took forever to heal. Even after that, Lisa was never one to talk about adverse experiences. She put a positive spin on everything. School was always great…she was always happy and unfailingly popular. That was her story and she stuck to it.

We went to a train station one cold autumn morning to pick up a visitor coming to see us. I recall my father once telling me that in these modern times of 1963, all the trains had diesel engines. But that day I saw a steam engine before it was retired for good. I still recall the coal smoke and the pistons releasing their air pressure in fits and starts, slowly at first, and then gathering speed. "Pshush! Pshush! Pshush-pshush-pshush-pshush!" The smoke ejected in puffs from the smokestack at the front of the train, a sooty, black iron monster replete with pistons, pipes, and twisting metallic snakes.

INTRODUCING THE TOILETS

newport and Germany were largely about toilets. It was where my sister and I finished our toilet training. It was not done gently. Slaps were the order of the day for accidents. That may be why we generated so much bathroom humor. It helped dispel anxiety.

That is why there will always be jokes about the military, the police, money, sex, death, and toilets. In our case, it started off very primitively. "Poo-Poo! Wee-Wee!" followed by gales of laughter. Lisa had a sky-blue plastic baby potty; mine was white. Hers was a prettier color. She proudly called it her "summer potty" because it was the color of the Welsh summer sky. Mine was an uninteresting shade of off-white, and had no name. I preferred to use the small potty, though, instead of the adult commode, which appeared so enormously massive to me in my smallness. It had its gaping dark hole at nose level with a rushing, swirling whirlpool that I assumed could suck me in down its pipes to an unknown dark world with just the pull of a silver handle.

Many years later, I worked temporarily in a child development center. It had kid-sized toilets low to the ground. I smiled. Some adult had finally understood.

In those days, toilets flushed loudly. If it was because Welsh and German toilets simply have terrific water pressure or if my hearing was more acute in those days, I am not certain. My mother was utterly scornful of me holding my ears with one hand and flushing with the other. "Don't be so sensitive," she would snap. She sometimes admonished me, "Don't be scared of everything. Don't be such a crybaby."

Eventually, I started to hear the message, "Don't be..." And that stuck.

When I set off for kindergarten at a British army base school, I carried a deep fear of messing in my pants. I was horrified of what might happen if it were to transpire in the classroom in front of all the other children! The worst of scenarios occurred to me: *They would laugh or recoil in horror and nobody would want to be friends with me forever and ever. And my mother would finally abandon me once and for all.* I was, after all, constantly on the brink of flunking childhood.

These fears were what made me laugh at the bathroom humor that was ubiquitous in those days. A precocious little boy playing with me in a corner of the classroom said, "I know a nursery rhyme." He pointed at my chest and then my rear end, reciting, "Milk, milk, lemonade, 'round the corner fudge is made."

Later, in elementary school, I heard the story of another little boy who asked the teacher if he could use the restroom. She said, "Say your alphabet first." So he went, "ABCDEFGHIJKLMNO...QRSTUVWXYZ." The teacher asked, "Where's the P?" He answered, "It's running down my legs!"

I remained curious for a long time about the fascinating world behind the door of the Boys' Toilet. I never dared enter, but I watched the young males in my class going in and out, wondering what marvels they were experiencing inside. Finally, one day after school, I finally mustered all of my courage and pushed open the door...what a letdown that was. Except for that pear-shaped piece of plumbing on the wall, which I soon found out about, it looked exactly like the girls' bathroom. Curiosity satisfied, I lost all interest in what was going on in the boys' restroom.

Toilet issues were our greatest fears in those days, but humor helped. In dealing with our bodily functions, we made fun of them and eventually got used to them.

It was freeing, years later, to chat to a young mother in a women's restroom and hear her tell me that her five-year-old girl, like me at that age, held her ears when she flushed. "That toilet must sound really loud to their sensitive ears," she smiled. I was relieved. At age 55, I finally knew I wasn't a freak. Her little boy reminded me of myself in another way, too. After I went into one of the cubicles and began attending to business, I heard the mother say, "Josh, stop looking under the bathroom stalls!"

On some level, I had expected our lives in Newport to last forever. I did not yet know that everything changes and ends. Even the stony, sooty, cold, mountainous land of Wales with Brenda, its other towering adults, giant black posts, whistling steam trains, and, yes, toilets, eventually became memories instead of everyday realities.

13

THE NEVER₀RUTHLESS RUTH

m y joy was pure and all encompassing when I met Ruth. She was Brenda's successor—our new nanny. She came to us just before we left Newport and went with us to Germany in the mid-1960s. The first day I looked upon her foolish but gentle smile, her wiry, messy brown hair, her tall slender figure, and the apron she always wore, I saw that she looked happy. Instinctively, I knew that Ruth, even with her intellectual deficits, would never be unkind.

Ruth was an angel. A foolish angel, to be sure. She had an IQ that was barely average, which meant that she not only took care of us, she played with us as if she were another child. She had endless ideas for games and activities for us to do together. She taught me how to draw a picture and then cut it out with scissors. I was four years old and proud of this accomplishment. "That's VERY good!" Ruth praised me as I held up a ragged-edged stick figure of myself I had just cut out. I recall us playing The Beatles on the new stereo in the living room, and Ruth and Lisa and I dancing and clapping together, and giggling. Oh, how we all giggled.

Ruth's family was bizarre. Her mother, whom I met only once, talked to herself and seemed to see things I did not, like a large rabbit in the corner. Ruth had a friend named Mrs. Lappin who was also weird, but in a good way. She was always pleased to see us. What I remember most is that her gray hair stood up in tufts, resembling scrubby grass on a West Texas ranch. She was always pulling and tugging at her hair. No wonder it stood straight up. Mrs. Lappin would greet us at the door and immediately begin by saying, "Ooo!" followed by unintelligible rapid-fire speech accompanied by cookies. We accepted the gibberish as the price of the cookies. For all of her insanity, Mrs. Lappin was a fine baker.

Ruth clapped her hands at every drawing of a doggie, horsy, and kitty that we made and gave her. She hung them up all over her bedroom. I wish Ruth were still around today. I would like to come home from work after a hard day and see Ruth there, clapping and cheering me just for showing up. When I manage to tie my shoes without them coming undone, I want her there approving this startling accomplishment. "That's VERY good!" Perhaps Mrs. Lappin can be there too, wagging her arms around in praise, passing around cookies, and exclaiming "Ooo!"

Soon after Ruth came to care for us, my mother expected to return to Gary, Indiana. Instead, my father took another consulting assignment in Dortmund, Germany. Again, I knew nothing of the fierce marital fights over that move other than my mother had pointed out that my father had prom-ised to return to the United States. My father's response was that things had changed. He loved my mother, but not enough to give up working overseas. My mother depended on him for the income, so she went along.

Later, I did overhear their late night marital spats. My mother declared many times to my father, "I hate you!"

I loved Dortmund. My childhood memories include brightly colored playgrounds that the engineering-minded Germans had built. I was also enchanted by the streetcars. They had their own separate miniature traffic lights with tiny red, orange, and green. Riding the streetcar into downtown Dortmund for ice cream was a much-anticipated treat. I loved anything small and shiny in those days, and riding the tram and watching those tiny lights suited me. In those days, I appreciated small things because every-thing appeared large. Adults were big. I had to look up to see my parents' faces. The furniture was high. The steps leading up to the house were steep. And once again, my worries about giant toilets reappeared. German toilets were, if anything, even louder than Welsh ones. I had the same concerns about falling in and being sucked into oblivion. So the tiny traffic lights for the streetcar were a comfort to me.

While I loved Dortmund, my mother did not. She complained about the ugly industrial town. She complained about the gray house we lived in and the gray air we breathed. Actually, we had been led to understand that we would live in the entirely gray house. It turned out that we only lived in the downstairs part of the gray house; the upstairs was occupied by our landlady, Frau Koehlen. (That is "Mrs. Koehlen" for those who speak no German). Frau Koehlen was a lady about whom I remember almost nothing…except for a farewell letter in broken English she gave us when we moved. She wanted to say a kind farewell to both my mother and my father. "Betty, I wish much success to you and your haspbend," it read.

The state of Dortmund household technology was primitive. When we needed hot water, we had to run it into tanks mounted above the kitchen sink and bathtub. The water took ten minutes to heat up. Once it was hot, the red light on the front of the tank went off. It took forty minutes to have enough hot water for a bath. When my mother first walked into the house and saw the state of the plumbing, she sat down and cried. Never mind that she missed her kinfolks. At that moment, she missed her hot water faucet and dishwasher. She also missed her piano.

My mother was a fine pianist and had gotten her degree at Indiana University in music education. She traded hot water, dishwasher, piano, and kinfolks for mounted wall tanks and freely flowing German beer. The beer made the trade off easier. She learned to drink more, although she never caught up with my father.

To add to my mother's stress, Ruth's mental challenges proved to be an issue in Germany. She never learned to speak German and struggled to be understood when my mother sent her to the grocery store. She took on the manner of a frightened baby deer in the woods. One evening, Ruth went out with a boyfriend she had met at her German class. When she got home, we were all out. Ruth had forgotten her key. It was raining. She stood in the rain and got progressively wetter and colder.

Later, when we got home, I saw her with her head down on the wooden dressing table, crying in our bedroom. It was weird to see an adult crying. Even when President Kennedy got shot, my mother had told me about it with anguish in her voice, but she didn't cry. I had no idea before that night that adults ever cried. Poor Ruth could have gone to the tavern down the street, but she did not think to do that. She left us soon after to go home to her family, while Dad shook his head about someone "not having enough sense to come in out of the rain."

14

ADJUSTING TO GERMANY

After Ruth left, our mother took over full responsibility for our care. We had shopping trips with her on Saturdays where she got groceries at a store called *Karstadt*. I loved this German store. We bought *bratwurst* and *knockwurst* there, and also *Butterkase* and *Hollanderkase*. *Bratwurst* has been blasphemed these days. Even 7-11 sells "brats," which makes me cringe. Anyway, when I announced how much I loved *Hollanderkase* (Dutch cheese) Lisa defiantly spoke up and declared that *Butterkase* was much better. But that's the kind of thing Lisa did. Her life commandment was, "Never be like my sister."

At the store, I also scoped out the German detergent brands with their brightly colored boxes: Aktiv, Omo, and Persil. I tried to persuade my mother to try a new brand every time we went to *Karstadt*. My mother, being my mother, always bought the brand that was cheapest. Trips to and from the grocery store were places where I processed my initial culture shock. How strange it was in those days to find that I could no longer understand the neon signs above the shops. A drug store was an *Apotheka*. A street was a *StraBe*, which I called a "strah-buh" until I found out that what looked like an oddly shaped letter B was a double S and was pronounced *Strasse*.

So many German words seemed impossibly long. I now know that compound words exist in most languages, but German's grammar construction in particular lends itself to easily attaching parts to make single words stretch across a page. As a result, the language has terminology that on a human body would be called obese. As Mark Twain put it, "Some German words are so long that they have perspective." Not all words were as long as *Rechtsschutzversicherungsgesellschaften*, which means "insurance companies providing legal protection" but to a five-year-old, many were overwhelming. I learned about the umlaut, the two dots on top of vowels that flattened the sound. An "o" with an umlaut on top was pronounced *eu*. My age favored me for learning German. Young children have fluid brains for acquiring languages, and Lisa and I learned passable German by playing with the children across the street, Eva and Hubert (pronounced e-VA and hu-BERT, stress on the second syllable). I only wish we had stayed in Germany longer so I could have acquired a permanent fluency.

I was not the only one who struggled with culture shock and language barriers. Unbeknownst to me, but very well "knownst" to my mother, after I went to school and Dad went to work, she was stuck trying to get the house painting and repairs done by working with German painters and plumbers. It was enormously stressful to talk to these workmen with a dictionary in one hand, using the other one to gesture and make hand signals in a kind of high-stakes game of charades.

One evening we were on a family car trip in our white Ford Taunus, the car named for a German mountain range north of Frankfurt. We had traveled a long way and we were all hungry and exhausted. We had passed several towns that whispered their tempting promises of food and *Apfelsaft* (apple juice), but Dad had his heart set on one sizable town that he swore was just ahead. Lisa and I had begun to whimper and whine. Dad said, "No need to worry. We're near that town. I've seen a lot of signs for it. It's called *Umleitung*." We drove for several more miles and saw another sign for *Umleitung*. Then another further along. Finally, Mom picked up her omnipresent German/English dictionary and looked it up. She found that *Umleitung* meant *detour*. We went on, leaving the previous towns behind. One of Dad's cardinal rules on car trips was, "We never backtrack."

Mom and Dad each also flunked their German driving test by one point. They thought that since they were so close to passing, they might be allowed to get licenses. But no dice. The instructor was a stern old man, a Nazi alumni who didn't like Americans, or so my parents told me. My parents had to go back to driving school to learn to read road signs. I bet my mother got even more homesick for Normalville in those days.

I found a lot to love about Dortmund. First and foremost, I was safe from Brenda's slaps forever, or so I thought. And I turned out to be right. She could have crossed the English Channel to visit us, but never did. Second, the *Konditorei*, or bakery-café, remains a heavenly memory: a place of sweets, cakes, conversational time with my mother, and the aromatic smells of coffee and German hot chocolate. I have heard it said that smells are our most indelible memories. Seeing and smelling the cocoa (*warm Schokolade*) flow out of the silver spout of the pot was pure, happy anticipation. I love coffee shops to this day. The sight of decorated cakes and cookies conjures fantasies of perpetual vacation and a sugar-induced sense of well-being.

I clearly remember my first day of kindergarten. I was enrolled in a British army base school called Victoria Primary School. My teacher's name was Miss Birnie. She was Scottish, of course, with a name like that. But she had a very English accent. She looked old to me. She was about thirty-five, and had prematurely gray hair and thick glasses. I suppose every child thinks her teachers look old, but Miss Birnie really did look older than her years. With the gray hair and glasses, brown sweaters, tweed skirts, stockings and brown-laced shoes, she looked fifty. When she was fifty, she looked seventy. She was younger than my father, but was once mistaken for his mother. I am sure she found it tiresome.

She had a knack for working with children. She managed to get us excited about learning phonics by creating ladders out of chalk on the blackboard, and each time we made the correct sound that corresponded to the right letter, we moved higher and higher up the ladder. If we hesitated too long, Miss Birnie would playfully shake the pointer in her hand to communicate, "You're going to fall!" and then if the child did not produce the right sound, down went the pointer to the bottom of the blackboard and Miss Birnie called out "Aaah!" Then she gave the right answer and the student had to begin again, naming each letter's sound.

She even got me interested in mathematics with her brightly colored flash cards, showing basic equations. It was one of the few times I was interested in or good at math.

15

FAMILY FESTIVALS OF FUN

When I wasn't at school, the holidays were superb. My father loved his job, but he also loved being a father. He loved that role so much that instead of saying, "I said," he would say to us, "Dad said." He referred to himself in the third person, as Dad.

It is only now after he has been dead nine years that I realize how lucky we were. In my current job at the Austin State Hospital, I have heard many tales of neglectful, abusive, and absent fathers. My own father played the role with zest. Although he was slightly drunk most of the time, and very drunk sometimes, he fathered us with devotion. I didn't realize the dimensions or depth of my father's drinking until years later. I once thought my father could not be an alcoholic, because I had never seen him drunk. I now know I never saw him sober. Yet he did so much for us. It's miraculous that he pulled it off.

I recall my father clearest during Christmas seasons, and particularly Christmas of 1964. At five years old, I can still see in my mind's eye the endless tangled strings of Christmas lights in the living room. I see my father patiently untangling them. If one light went out, they all went out, and he had to figure out where the loose or burned out bulb was and fix it. After fourteen years of marriage, he had gotten handy with this sort of thing. My mother claimed that when they were dating, he wanted to get in bed with her so badly that he lied about what a great handyman he was. If so, he remedied that deficiency quickly. Perhaps my mother threatened to withhold sex unless he started doing home repairs.

Anyway, with no cursing that I ever heard, he rigged endless strings of Christmas lights and as a family we decorated the tree, a delicious-smelling evergreen spruce, which my parents struggled with in order to stuff it into the tree stand. When decorated, the spirals of gold tinsel, silken ornament balls, and pixies in striped jumpsuits sitting on the branches made me sure Santa would be pleased. The memories of piles of gifts under the tree, twinkling tiny lights, and our absolute faith in the reality of Santa amounted to a magic that no Christmas I ever had as an adult could ever match.

Some of the lights shone in multicolored splendor while others blinked on and off. Dad played German Christmas carols on the stereo. I still play the CD of *Stille Nacht, Heilige Nacht* by the *Bielefeld Kinderchor* (the German town of Bielefeld's children's choir) that my father once owned on vinyl. I am hopelessly biased, but I still think it's beautiful. No later rendition of *In Dulce Jubilo* that I've heard comes close to those children's harmonic young voices. I see the flashing, twinkling Christmas tree lights synchronized with Bielefeld music as a snapshot of the perfect fairy-tale Christmas. Later, encountering lights and music with a disco ball synchronized with the Village People singing "Macho Man," I thought that the lights and music were much better with Bielefeld.

We left milk and cookies for Santa, of course. My mother, my sister, and I solemnly laid out the full glass and several freshly baked Toll House goodies. The next morning, after opening the gifts, we found a note written in large block capital letters. "Dear Ann and Lisa, Thank you for the milk and cookies. It was very kind of you to leave them for me. I gave the milk to my reindeer for our long journey on the sleigh. Donder and Blitzen especially enjoyed it." My father got very imaginative with those notes each year.

There was one major disaster that threatened to ruin Christmas in 1964. The steam radiator behind the Christmas tree leaked one night after my sister and I had gone to bed. There was a roaring noise, and hot water squirted and hit the tree. Tree, tinsel, ornaments, and pixies fell with a crash. Somehow Dad fixed it. Then he assembled a child-sized grocery store complete with toy cash register, miniature boxes and cans of food, and tiny fruits and vegetables made out of German marzipan candy. There was even a red plastic phone on the store shelf. Dad put it all together with wrenches, screwdrivers, and the help of some dinner guests who were visiting that night. They got drunk along with Dad, and refused to go home. So Dad told them he had to assemble the toy grocery store and they would have to help. They did. After all that work, they were thankful to go home.

That Christmas, with its glistening tree, shining ornaments, blinking lights, twisting tinsel, red stockings hung by a real fireplace, carols playing out of two stereo speakers (stereo was new back then and two separate speakers was a novelty), miniature toy grocery store, and the story of the exploding radiator was both fairytale enchantment and the spoiler for every Christmas thereafter. No Yuletide since has ever measured up.

In those days, Dad could fix, smooth over, or build anything. There is still part of me that thinks he might come back and work his magic once more. I would like him to knock on the door and pay me a brief visit. Just five minutes, so I could thank him.

16

MORE LIFE WITH DAD

received a Magic Eight Ball for Christmas from Dad that year—a gift that kept on giving for years. The Magic Eight Ball was a black sphere just like the eight ball on a pool table. It had a floating plastic polygon that turned different directions with answers to yes and no questions written on each surface. If you asked the Magic Eight Ball a question and then turned it over, you would see a response on the plastic triangle below. For example:

"Magic Eight Ball, will I marry a rich man when I grow up?"

The wondrous ball might reply, "It is decidedly so."

"Will I be pretty?"

"Yes, definitely."

"Will it rain tomorrow?"

"Reply hazy. Try again."

"Will I have ice cream for supper?"

"No."

I think this nifty gift made me comfortable with asking inanimate objects questions. For me, the Magic Eight Ball was the precursor to Google. A magical place willing to give a reply to any question imagined… even open-ended ones. (A girlfriend told me that she googled Google and everything came up).

Technology has had such an influence in our lives over the last fifty years. My grandparents could never have imagined everything from digital

TV to computers to cellphones... I can visualize trying to explain it to Grandma Miller and her responding, "I never heard tell of such a thing."

Dad could be as carefree as a child and had an endless imagination. For example, when snow arrived and covered our backyard with three glistening white inches, Dad played a game with us called Fox and Geese. He was the fox, and we were the geese. He had to run after us in the footprints we made ahead of him. We screamed with delight as he pursued us. When he caught one of us, he would pick us up and swing us around.

I once asked him why he always cut a hole in the tip of his cigar. As Dad usually did, he gave a truthful answer and then embellished it. "Because cigars don't have filters like cigarettes do," he explained. You cut a hole so you can puff on the cigar. If that hole isn't there, you could end up sucking so hard that your ears fall off."

Dad could also make up stuff out of thin air better than anyone I ever met. Often, I did not know whether he was telling the truth or spinning a tall tale, and I still wonder whether he knew the difference himself. A counselor I went to years later, when I told him about the stories Dad told and actions he'd taken, said that my father had a hard time distinguishing reality from fantasy.

But it is only natural for a child to believe everything her father says and it wasn't until I was older that I began to question his statements. One of his stories was about a prudish woman he claimed to know. He mimicked the hysterical phone call she'd made to the police. "There's a man undressing right in front of my window!"

When the cops came, they said, "We don't see the man."

The woman said, "Oh, you can't see him from here. You have to stand on this chair!"

Dad's good humor didn't only apply to his storytelling. He had a way of being optimistic in the face of disappointment, which bordered on the ludicrous. One time when he was behind by a massive number of points in a Six-Tricks card game, my mother said with a sad smile, "I think we're losing, honey."

Dad looked thoughtful for a moment and then raised his chin up high. "It's always darkest before the dawn," he announced. This unwarranted optimism was so indicative of Dad's personality and he applied it to serious as well as light-hearted situations.

As a teenager, Lisa started having struggles with obesity, which led to abusing prescription pills, drinking, and school failure, Dad met her one morning on the stairs. He gave her one of his wet slobbery kisses and declared, "You're getting better and better every day!"

In a similar situation after our fifth move, I was struggling with depression associated with being in a developing country while trying to adjust to the ways of an American Catholic school. The culture was vastly different from the London girls' prep school and British army base schools I had attended, Dad encouraged me as he so often had before, saying, "The world's your oyster!"

He said that one phrase more often than anything else. I still don't know exactly what it meant, but the way he said it sounded like I should be able to pull the world out of a shell and gulp it down. I know he meant well, but it never rang true. As I matured, I came to understand that wishing things were true does not make it so. As the old saying goes, "If wishes were horses, we'd all have a stable full."

We had a word for Dad's not-so-wise adages. We called them "Daddages." Even with my skepticism, I harbored a secret fantasy in the furthest corner of my heart until the day he died that somehow, some way, my father would make everything all right again. War, racism, poverty, even allergies and car trouble would one day be made okay once Dad got around to it. When Dad died, that was the hardest piece to let go of for me.

The blurred line between reality and fantasy was something Dad learned from his own father, my Grandpa Locasio. An example of his storytelling was when he told us about the man our oldest cousin planned to marry. The family did not like the man and Grandpa dreaded meeting him.

"I went and *throwed up* three times before I could come downstairs and say 'glad to meet ya,'" Grandpa said as he shared his version of the story.

"Now *Grandpa!* You know you didn't do that!"

But Grandpa half-believed he did. He constructed his own version of reality after the fact.

Grandpa often said that when my father was a boy, he left Grandpa scrawled notes that read, "No Mun. No Fun. Your Son."

Grandpa said he'd answer them with, "Too Bad. Too Sad. Your Dad!"

Grandma chimed in as always with, "Grandpa!" and told him to stop fibbing to us kids.

Grandpa would make all kinds of things up. For example, when we were teenagers he came to visit us and on the way to Ohio stopped and ate at Perkins Pancake. When he arrived at our house he told us he had stopped at "Turpin's Topcake."

So my father was just doing what he had learned as a kid—how to fabricate stories, and how to get a reaction from your spouse.

17

THEN THERE WAS MOM...AGAIN

In the early days of living in Germany, I still carried a security blanket around. In the days of Brenda Jones, I went to bed every night clutching the blanket like a shield and hoping for magical protection from being slapped the next day. I called my blanket "Little Darling." At the time, I did not know why I chose that name. I now think that that was what I wanted to be in my mother's eyes. It was not to be. My mother resented being overseas and overruled on her desire to return home. She never realized how eagerly, and with so little success, I sought her good opinion.

We lived in an apartment in later years where we had to contend with "neighbors from hell." Old Mrs. Cohen, who lived in the apartment directly below us, did not like children. She loathed it when we played in front of the building, walking on the wall there near her living room window. We liked walking on that wall. She liked spying on us. The wall was about three feet high and just wide enough to challenge us to keep our balance while stepping along it. We had contests to see who could walk along it the fastest. Whenever Mrs. Cohen saw us or heard us laugh, she would shout out her window at us, "Go away! Play in the park!"

Mom dealt with Mrs. Cohen by telling me, "You shouldn't play outside the building anyway. I think it ruins the look of a building when children play outside it." That was how I learned that if I appeared in front of a building, it became ugly.

My mother did not suffer fools gladly, and as a young child I often looked and acted foolish. One time when I fell down and scraped my knee, she said, "You should have seen the crack in the sidewalk. It's stupid not to look where you're going."

My slow physical development earned reprimands. She was furious when at four-years-old I walked down steps by putting both feet on a step. "One foot on each step! Not two at a time!" she would scold.

"Why can't you ride a bicycle like Nicky?" she demanded as she pointed out to me how our neighbor, Eleanor's young granddaughter, rode her two-wheeler with speed and grace. I watched Nicky's long brown hair flowing in the wind as she sped by, knowing that I could no more do that than I could fly to the moon. "Look at that. She does it so well. What's wrong with you?"

She also despaired over how long it took me to learn to tie my shoe-laces. "Make a loop! Wrap the lace around it! Stick it through the other loop!" The angrier she became, the less I achieved. "You should do better. I'm so disappointed in you."

All her friends' children learned to jump rope, tie shoelaces, and ride bikes long before I did. It caused my mother a great loss of status among her peers. She often reminded me of that.

At the age of nine, I finally learned to ride a bike. It was a warm spring day in the park where all the children played. I was straddled across a bike belonging to a girl named Julia. I sat on the seat with one foot on the pedal, the other on the ground. "Well, are you going to do something or not?" demanded Michael, a boy given to sarcasm and jeering.

"It's no good. She can't do it," declared the blond-haired Julia as she tossed her long tresses back.

The other kids just stood around and watched. I felt sweat tickle the back of my neck. I took a few deep breaths. Then I pushed off. I pressed the pedal down. Then the other one. I felt the wind blowing in my face as I gained speed and left Michael and Julia and the others far behind.

Exultant, I finished circling the park before returning the bike to Julia. Then I ran in to tell my mother. She was sitting on the living room couch, smoking her cigarette when I entered. "Mom! I can ride a bike!" I jumped up and down.

Mom took a long inward drag and the end of the cigarette glowed orange. She exhaled smoke and then shrugged. "It should have happened a long time ago."

Mom had few sources of self-esteem other than her children, so my failure to deliver physical accomplishments was a serious blow to her ego. Others in her life contributed to her lack of confidence. A boss she worked for several years earlier, once told her, "Betty, you are an amazing secretary. If you were a man, I'd put you in management. Since you're a woman, I can't do that."

Statements like that were devastating. My mother adored all things about money and commerce. She could have been an expert, hard-headed businesswoman. My godmother Aunt Gloria, Mom's best friend, later told me that Mom was one of the best secretaries U.S. Steel had ever employed. She could manipulate columns of figures with ease and taught herself bookkeeping. She was a woman before her time, forced to be a housewife and mother.

Later in life, Mom's favorite "indoor sport" was watching the stock market ticker tape. After she had hip surgery at the age of 70, her first groggy, mumbled words to us when she came out of anesthesia were, "How'd the market do today?" Many times she told us, "If I hadn't had you kids, I could have been a top secretary. If I hadn't had you kids, I could work. And make money. Which we need. Because you kids cost me a lot of money. And I wouldn't have to stay home. I could travel more with your father."

Even with the chastisements, I still cherish the bright spots of the early days. They were just as real as what my mother told me. After all, I had the delights of the Tooth Fairy and Santa and neither of them visited children poorer than we were; we were blessed by having both. The arrival of a shiny coin under my pillow eased the discomfort of wiggling a tooth until it fell out and tasting metallic blood in my mouth. I never caught my parents' Tooth-Fairying, either. They were clever about knowing whether I was sleeping or not.

And Christmases in later years, although never as magical as the one in 1964, were still special. Santa Claus came every year until I was nine. My parents enjoyed Santa so much that they kept the myth going as long as possible. I started asking why the magical old elf couldn't bring me everything on my Christmas list every year, since it was all done by magic and he had so many elves working for him. Mom told me that I wanted so many toys, she had to start paying him. Mom, always the businesswoman, eventually went into business with Santa.

Unaware of all of the reasons for my mother's short temper and frequent outbursts of anger, I clutched my blanket, Little Darling, for a long time. I held onto it for a while in Germany, but by then it was close to being worn out from so much clutching and washing. It finally fell apart. I recall seeing it with balls of white cotton stuffing hanging out.

I was able to let it go without too much regret.

18

DAD'S TALLEST TALE AND DEEPEST SECRET

my father, when he wasn't drinking, found novel ways to entertain two restless little girls when the family ate at a restaurant. In those days, people actually expected children to behave in restaurants, but we were as energy-laden as most youngsters. One night, while we waited in a restaurant for what seemed like an eternity for our food, we started our usual whine. "When, oh when will our food get here? Oh when, oh when will that be?" We sang it in a whiny, singsong voice that was calculated to annoy our elders to the maximum extent possible.

My father realized he had to entertain us somehow. He turned to us. "Just be glad you're not eating at the Old Slop House."

We were intrigued. "Daddy, what's the Old Slop House?"

"Ask me some questions, and I'll tell you."

"Okay. Who waits on you at the Old Slop House?"

"Nobody. When you come in, all the waiters and waitresses sit down, and *you* wait on *them*."

"What's on the menu at the Old Slop House?"

"There's no menu. Before they open for dinner, they slop everything they've cooked on the walls. You go up and down each wall and taste everything, then you know what to order."

My father also told us true stories of how he was a waiter at a restaurant called Kelly's, when he was thirteen. This was the era of the Great

Depression. He began as a dishwasher, and worked his way up to waiter. With his earnings, he bought his mother a couch. The family needed the money. His father had been laid off from the stone mill almost as soon as the economic crash occurred in 1929. I can imagine that the Old Slop House stories were invented by a young man who had been on his feet for hours. He probably grinned inwardly at the thought of slopping the food all over the walls. And how attractive it must have seemed to imagine a restaurant where the customers became the waiters, and he the one served.

The full name of the restaurant where Dad worked was Kelly's Lunch Counter. It burned down when Dad was in his late teens. He never told me that. I found it out decades later by reading online historical archives from Upperville. I wonder why such a significant event as the burning of one's place of work never came up in conversations with Dad? But that's how it went. Dad repeated himself endlessly with his favorite stories, his platitudes, his "Daddages." But other important events were never mentioned. I wonder if he was happy when it burned. It was his first job, and his hardest. Or maybe he had moved on another job by then, so the burning of Kelly's held little significance.

My father was a man of many secrets. I discovered one of them by accident when I found a song he'd composed at the university music school before switching to a business major. It was called "Betty and Me." I thought it was a great tribute to my mother. I loved the line, "I long for the day, when two will be three, Happy together, that's Betty and Me." I asked him why he didn't sing it to Mom when he played his guitar. He shrugged his shoulders, said he didn't know, and changed the subject. Years later, I found out that this was a love song to his first wife—who was also named Betty. She dumped him while he was overseas in the Navy and married someone else. Aunt Rose told me later that Dad got a "Dear John" breakup letter from Betty the First, which is what such an epistle was called.

I saw the first Betty's photo in Dad's high school yearbook while we were visiting at the house of his school friend, Velma. Betty was a plain, nondescript woman. She was not nearly as beautiful, aristocratic, or glamorous as my mother. Or maybe that's just my bias showing. I asked Velma, "Why doesn't Dad ever say anything about this lady?"

Velma smiled and shook her head. "I think it hurts him."

That was just one of Dad's secrets. He had others that I discovered later. But the secret about Dad's first wife was my mother's secret too. Neither one of them ever mentioned it to me. That was something else my mother carried with her.

Was it hard for her to be Betty the Second?

19

SISTERLY SHENANIGANS

Dad was secretive, Mom was angry, but it was with Lisa that I spent the most time. My sister never forgave me for being born first. To some extent we were destined to be natural rivals. We were only fourteen months apart, both girls, raised as a single unit, and expected to share everything. We were sometimes mistaken for twins. Lisa hated that. She wanted to be different from me in every way.

We competed with each other from our earliest days. If I won or was praised for something, she counted it as a loss for her. And vice versa. The prize for which we contended was our parents' love. Mom facilitated the process. She believed that if she fostered competition, we would spur each other on to do our best. She would tell me, "Look, Lisa's vocabulary is getting bigger. You need to work on that too!" Then to my sister she would say, "Lisa, Ann has such a slim figure. She's so thin and pretty. You should be like that too!"

I was slender in those days, with shiny, silky brown hair and brown eyes. Lisa was always, to her chagrin, a little on the plump side. She had dark wavy blond hair and green eyes. She was shorter than me, but immensely strong. I inherited my mother's tall, slender build, while Lisa's shorter, squat figure resembled my father's. So did her physical strength. When it came to a physical fight, she always won because she could hit so hard.

After she did, my mother would exhort me, "Fight back harder. You don't need to act so weak."

When she said this, Lisa was delighted. She soon learned a new vocabulary word. "You're a weakling," she declared triumphantly, celebrating her physical superiority and extensive vocabulary in one fell swoop.

But my slender figure pleased me, because it pleased my father. I wasn't strong, but I was thin and pretty and my father liked slender women. He liked them so much that my mother, after gaining a few post-pregnancy pounds after Hankley was born, started taking amphetamine diet pills to lose weight. My father approved. "Mom's getting so slim! And when she goes for a walk she has so much energy she almost skips down the street!"

My plump sister, meanwhile, drew pictures of skinny princesses and dreamed of being a ballerina. Unfortunately, she did not have any grace of movement. Even as a child, she didn't step. She stomped. Instead of excelling at ballet and dance, she became a comic and made us laugh by exaggerating her lack of grace.

Dad called me his "little princess." He called Lisa his "little dumpling."

Lisa and I dedicated our lives to defeating each other. I was the older kid who went to school while she didn't. Mom tried to get her into a preschool in Dortmund, but there were no spaces available in those postwar years. But Lisa found a creative way to deal with being left at home. I came home from the Victoria School one afternoon and Lisa began her tale. It became an ongoing narrative.

She grinned and began, "You'll never guess where I went last night. Somewhere special. To the kindergarten!" She fabricated a well-rehearsed story of how, after I fell asleep, she sneaked out and went to a special kindergarten at night. Her teacher's name was Miss Pearce. She had a best friend at kindergarten, a boy named Frank. They played a game with very high nets where everyone went up in balloons to hit the ball over the net. The name of the game was Wichita.

She got the idea from the *Wizard of Oz* about the balloons and the name of Wichita, as Wichita, Kansas was the Wizard's hometown.

Dorothy mentioned it in our children's *Wizard of Oz* record that we played constantly. Miss Pearce, the teacher, and the fictitious friend Frank were characters in one of her storybooks.

Lisa told me solemnly that they played the game of Wichita every night.

"Do you win prizes?" I asked.

"Yes," she nodded. "If you win, you win your lunch."

"What if you lose?"

"If you lose, you don't eat. But it's okay because I always win."

It was a tough system. Lisa competed for food in her fictitious kindergarten the way the two of us competed for love in real life. For every question I asked about this nightly kindergarten, she made up a reasonably credible answer. Finally, I began to ask her if I could go. I begged her. I pleaded with her.

She always said, "No." The midnight kindergarten and all of Lisa's adventures therein were her revenge on me. It was quite an intellectual achievement as Lisa was only four years old when she created her imaginary nocturnal kindergarten.

A more remarkable achievement was that Lisa taught herself to read before the following September rolled around. By the time Lisa got to Miss Birnie's real, daytime kindergarten, she was reading well above grade level and writing very well for her age. She was only five years old when she wrote a letter to my Grandpa and Grandma Miller before we flew across the Atlantic to see them on summer vacation:

Dear Grandma and Grandpa,

I am coming to America. I know that you adore me. I am willing to see you. This PAD of PAPER contains 100 pages if you would LIKE TO KNOW.

Love,
Lisa

One time, in a moment of inattention, she wrote to express her affection for her grandparents by telling them she loved them. In Lisa's earliest days, before she could write well, most of her letters said I Love You. Love Lisa. Once, in a moment of inattention she wrote, "Dear Grandma and Grandpa, I Love Lisa." (At the time I thought she was telling the exact truth.) Then there was the time she wrote her name in shaky capitals, L-I-S-A, but she left a stem off the capital A so it looked like a P. "Oh look!" she exclaimed. "I wrote L-I-S-P! That isn't LISA. It's LEESPEE!" And she dissolved into volleys of giggles.

Anything, no matter how inane, could be funny in those days. Vainly her elders tried to tell her the word was "lisp." To her it was always "Leespee" and the word "pee" was enough to send her into hysterics. I once read that children laugh about a hundred times a day. This kind of thing is why.

Reading Lisa's letters, I saw how she measured herself against me. "I know how to ride a bike. Ann Lee does not know how yet," she declared in a triumphant letter to my grandparents at age seven. When I finally learned to ride a bike, she immediately lost interest in riding bikes at all. Its value was only to prove her superiority.

She had another quirk. When she played games with me, she refused to let us keep score. When in frustration I asked her why, she said, "Because if I lose, you'll say ha-ha-ha." Losing to me in a game carried too much risk when the prize to be lost was a parent's love. Life was a zero-sum game. If I won, she lost. If she succeeded, I failed. If I looked good, she looked bad. That was our world view.

The rivalry started young, ran deep, and persisted over many years. We both learned early on that someone else's success was a threat and meant that we had failed in some way. Someone else's achievement diminished us. Worst of all, to Lisa, was her sister's achievement and vice versa. This became a prototype for other people's success. It took years for me to learn to wish others well. It was a great and liberating day when I finally got over myself.

Lisa outperformed me in making many friends. She learned early that jokes about poop and farting were hilarious to her classmates. She developed the ability to fake a fart with her armpit. My mother would reprove her for talking about "poo-poo" at the table, but I would always giggle. She learned to suck air into her vagina and fart it out. I've never seen anyone else do that, but I don't ask if they can. "Excuse me, I was wondering if...?" It isn't the sort of thing I'd ask a stranger on a bus.

But we still had a great deal of fun. We explored our bodies. Adults forget that children's bodies don't come with owner's manuals. We once touched our tongues together. Tongues were for tasting, but we wondered what the tongue itself tasted like. Not much, as it happens, but that had to be learned. I once told Lisa I had eleven fingers, not ten. She counted my ten fingers. Then I held up a hand to her and counted backwards. "Ten, Nine, Eight, Seven, Six!" Then I held up my other hand. "Plus five is eleven!" I probably learned this sort of thing from Dad, who once told us he had "seven holes in his head." Then he pointed at his two eyes, two ears, two nostrils, and mouth.

Our active imaginations made for rich and varied pretend play. I recall our pretending to have a morning cocktail party. In Europe in those days, people held cocktail parties at eleven o'clock in the morning, so we were imitating what we were witnessing. My mother eventually adjusted to drinking martinis before noon. She even grew to like it. She never became an alcoholic, though. My father did.

In those days, Lisa and I watched the ladies, wives of my father's colleagues, coming to the house in cocktail dresses to drink sherry or other libations. We pretended to be our mother, serving the cocktails and talking about how dreadful the weather was—and in Wales and Germany, this usually was true. Clouds, rain, and chilly dampness were the norm, especially in Wales.

Lisa and I would chat with our imaginary guests about imaginary mutual friends and the horrible weather. We mimed pouring cocktails into miniature plastic cups. At one point in time, we were pretending that very few people had arrived, but that a crowd of guests was waiting on the doorstep. Lisa said, "Oh, there's the doorbell. That must be all the others." She pretended to open the door and said, "Good morning, all the others!"

Life with Lisa wasn't really that bad. We had a lot of fun together. And we each did our best to excel in every area of achievement. How could we not, when so much was at stake? And the rivalry yielded the stories of her nocturnal kindergarten. Visions of Lisa sneaking out of her bunk bed at night to go to kindergarten still make me smile. She made it all so real.

I wonder if, now that she's passed on into the next life, she might be on an astral plane somewhere being taught by Miss Pearce, hanging out with Frank, playing Wichita, and winning her lunch.

20

SCHOOL GETS REAL AND REAL HARD

The following year, Lisa started kindergarten and had no more need to make up stories about attending at night. I entered first grade with a new teacher, Miss Stokes. I did not like Miss Stokes. She also seemed terribly old, although later I heard she was about twenty-six.

The demands on a first grader were harder than they had been in kindergarten. When we had to weigh, measure, and record the weights of dry beans and peas on a scale, I asked to go to the restroom and did not come back for half an hour. I remember Miss Stokes' beehive hairdo towering over me, and her index finger wagging at me for this attempt at avoiding an assigned task.

We studied science by finding out what substances would dissolve in water and which would not. We learned this by first stirring lemonade powder into water. We got to drink it afterwards, which was a real treat. Then we dumped some wooden bricks into a plastic tub of water and stirred them. Surprise! They didn't disappear like the lemonade powder. That's where I learned the term "soluble."

It all seemed too hard. I became lethargic about the whole business and would stop working. Miss Stokes told me that if I did not work during class time, I would have to stay in and work at playtime. First grade was also when I started to find mathematics difficult. Even today, when I balance my checking account, I feel inwardly thankful that I will never again have to learn the "borrowing" function of subtraction and the "carrying" function of addition. With the advent of calculators and computers, I do not know if these techniques are still taught, but I imagine they are.

Mathematics provided no scope for imagination. The answers were right or they were not. In my case, usually not. I recall graded papers returned to me with vertical rows of red X's beside each sum. A red check mark meant correct, a red X meant incorrect. I remember the X's best. I still don't like red pens.

Miss Stokes constantly told me to work harder. At the end of the day, the children who had done all their work got "free choice," which meant they had some unstructured indoor playtime in recompense for their superior industriousness. I was never among the free choice crowd. I spent every last minute correcting badly done math papers or in the Science Corner, still weighing dried beans and peas and recording the results.

A few years later, I heard a surprising story about this woman who constantly cracked the verbal whip to get me to work harder. My old kindergarten teacher Miss Birnie was at our house. By now she had become a family friend. She told of knowing Miss Stokes at the British army base where they both lived at that time. She recounted, "I was always an early riser, but Muriel Stokes was not. I would have finished breakfast at the teachers' mess hall, and Muriel would be just coming down to get started, dragging her body across the room for a cup of coffee. She was so slow and lazy."

Muriel Stokes constantly tried to get me to work hard, yet Miss Birnie remembered her as sluggish. No wonder I laughed so loud when years later I heard the story of a tough high school history teacher talk about a colleague who… "Whenever we saw a movie in class, it meant that Mr. Conners had a hangover." Teachers are human, after all.

I also got in trouble for not doing my "news" correctly. The way we did our "news" was to draw a horizontal line, dividing a blank sheet of paper into two halves. On the top half, we drew a picture of something that had happened to us recently. On the bottom half, we wrote a paragraph describing the event. One day, I forgot to draw the line and was, "in deep trouble for my absentmindedness." That was British school in those days. There were many rules, and a child simply could not be too careful. It was so easy to be in violation. "You know perfectly well, Ann Lee Locasio, that you don't do your news like that!" thundered Miss Stokes, her finger pointed at me and her beehive hairdo tossing as she spoke.

I learned long multiplication and long division in fourth grade. Physics began in sixth grade, chemistry in seventh. I wonder how I ever did it. All my energy went into schoolwork; I had little left over for friendships and was mostly a loner. However, I was not alone when Tony Walmsley, another misfit kid with bulging blue eyes, greasy blond hair, and faded old clothes, jumped out at me from behind corners and screamed, "Yaaaaaargh!" Or when Brian Hodgson, a muscular bruiser of a black haired boy three grades above me, deliberately bumped into me in the playground when I wasn't looking. Which he did anytime he got the chance.

I fantasized about magical rescue, that someday soon I would climb to the top of a mountain and literally live on top of the world and witness spectacular sunsets every night. Or I would be claimed by a royal family and marry a prince. Or my bedroom contained a secret passageway to a magic kingdom under the floor, which I would find any day. I dreamed of a fairyland that existed in the place far below where the water in my bathtub drained. I looked down the drain hole sometimes, hoping for that happy land to appear. The ability to conceive of a magical world helped me cope with the one I was given.

I had time to daydream about such things in the school corridors. We were not allowed to converse with each other there. We hung up our coats, took off our boots and changed into indoor shoes in winter; then we walked between the classroom, gym, art room, and music room in silence.

Grandma Miller once came over to visit us from America. (I'm sure my father sent her money for the plane ticket). She noticed that as we walked down the hall, a friend of mine approached from the other way, but I did not greet her. My outgoing grandmother, a leader in the Methodist Church Women and the Zeta Beta local sorority, tried to give me a lesson on the importance of friendliness.

I told it like it was. "Grandma, in the corridors we aren't ever allowed a single speak." While I don't recall saying this, I read it in my grandmother's travel journal later.

She commented, "The way the British treat children takes my breath away."

21

FAMILY FUN AND FLASHBACKS

School being what it was, meant I was even more thankful when summer arrived than most of my peers. Every other summer I got a wonderful respite from the stresses of school. Overseas management consultants, including my father, got six weeks of "home leave" every two years. My mother and sister and I got a few weeks more than that. When school was over for the summer, the three of us flew across the Atlantic to the USA. I remember leaving Germany in 1965 for the first home leave. The airplane trip, which would have been long for adults, seemed an eternity to children.

There was no jet way back then. We climbed metallic steps into the cabin; they had ridges on them to prevent slipping in wet weather. The engines screamed in our ears as we climbed but I found that exciting, not frightening. Once we got inside, that was Lisa's and my cue to start fighting over who would get the window seat first. In those days, many of our disputes were solved with the drawing of straws and flipping of coins.

When the pilot revved up the engines for takeoff, it was a pure adrenaline rush. The runway streaking past my window, the ground dropping away, the view of clouds from above, were unforgettable. Other memories were smaller but no less indelible. The meals fitted into trays. There were miniature salt and pepper shakers for each person with tiny paper covers on top of each one. (The waste was incredible but nobody thought about that then). There were decks of playing cards with the airline logo on them. We even helped the "air hostesses," as they were called, to clear everyone's trays after lunch. They didn't mind the help, and we got to move around and dispel all that built-up child energy.

We eventually arrived at the airport in Indianapolis where we were greeted by our maternal grandparents, Grandpa and Grandma Miller, and our paternal grandparents, Grandpa Innocenzio (Inno) and Grandma (Violet) Locasio. They were joined by a welcoming party of aunts, uncles, and cousins. I remember being amazed that all these people were my family. It seemed like a massive crowd, as if we were The Beatles arriving for the *Ed Sullivan Show*. Up until then, I thought my "family" was my parents and a whole lot of people with British accents.

The eight weeks that followed were golden Indiana summer days, playing on grass and under oak trees. The backyards weren't fenced. We ran in and out of them, and up and down lots of back alleys.

Our grandparents spoiled Lisa and me rotten. Grandpa Locasio in particular was known to come to us with a dollar bill in each hand and say, "Here's a buck each. You can save it, or you can blow it." Naturally, we always chose to "blow it." Grandpa would have been disappointed if we had chosen otherwise.

After he heard, "Let's blow it, Grandpa!" we would pile into his blue Chevrolet and head for Hegg's Drugstore, which contained a vast array of colorful plastic toys, paper dolls, Barbie dolls, and candy. A dollar could buy a lot of loot in those days. We took full advantage of Grandpa's generosity. Occasionally, with the self-centeredness of children, we would ask Grandpa if we could spend more than a dollar. Grandpa would say, "Where do you think I get my money, out of a *pump*?" As a stonecutter, he made a decent income, but was cautious about giving too much to us at once.

He was always what Hoosiers called "a character." So was his wife. Once, in the 1950s, Grandpa was driving with Grandma. Grandma loved to dance, as did her daughter, my aunt Rose. Aunt Rose used to sneak out of the house against parental prohibitions to go dancing with her high school boyfriend Jack, the school's football hero. Her yearbook from junior year was full of classmates wishing her "good luck with Jack." (Her luck held. She married him after graduation and they went dancing through forty-plus years together). One evening, decades ago, Grandma and Grandpa were driving when she said, "Inno! Let's go over there! It's a dance place called BODY'S HOP! I wonder what kind of place Body is. And I love to dance the Hop!"

Grandpa brought her back to reality when he growled, "Violet, that's Body Shop."

There were occasionally times when this was reversed; Grandpa got it wrong and Grandma let him know it. She came home from the Kroger's grocery store one afternoon and hauled in full paper sacks from the trunk of her car. As she carried in a bag full of produce with peaches on top, Grandpa was curious as to whether the peaches were ripe and ready to eat. If so, he was going to sample one. But in his question about the peaches he used the wrong word. "Violet," he demanded, "Are them peaches raw?"

Grandma looked over at him with a long stare, and faked an innocent wide-eyed surprise. "Why no, Grandpa," she answered earnestly. "They're cooked! When have you ever seen me buying *raw peaches*?"

Grandma Locasio was a character in her own right, although next to the lively and often noisy antics of Grandpa, her own peculiarities were less noticeable. But they were there. When my cousins, Sandy and Mark, played their Led Zeppelin and REO Speedwagon vinyl records, Grandma would roll her eyes and say they were playing, "that Knock Down and Drag Out Music."

She was a hypochondriac who constantly had weird reactions in her body, which she freely shared. "Garlic makes me burp," she often informed us. "I can't drink tea, it makes my skin crawl." And I knew never to ask Grandma a question when she first got up. "I can't do anything 'til I've had my coffee," she would tell me, loading up the metal basket in her coffee percolator with coffee grounds. I listened as the coffee percolated for several minutes, mesmerized by the pot. I can still hear the sound; few people today know the sound of coffee percolating. Until the coffee was perked and poured, I read a book or played until Grandma downed her first cup and metamorphosed into a conversationalist. After she died in 1998, her daughter Rose went through her enormous medicine closet and found prescription bottles dated 1984. It may have been taking a plethora of pills from two decades earlier that caused her to have all those weird bodily reactions. When she came to see us, she had to carry a separate suitcase to hold all the bottles of Maalox, her favorite laxative. When my father died, we found a similar laxative stash. *Like mother, like son.* He was as anal-retentive as she was.

Grandpa's heart was generally in the right place. He often declared to us, "I love ya like a hog loves slop." Once, we were all riding in the car to visit my aunt and uncle. I was a teenager who experimented with makeup with varying degrees of success. As I was applying a bright pink lip gloss, Grandpa chuckled. "Sweetie, even manure would look good on your lips." Grandpa always meant well. Although I snorted with derision at the time, I understood the intent.

Years later, after my sister died, I had a vivid dream that Grandpa was with my sister, my brother, and me sitting at their 1950s stainless steel and curvaceous Formica kitchen table. He was pointing his index finger at us and saying, "I may not have been the best gramps in the world, but I sure did love you kids." It sounded so much like him, it was as if he had come back to remind us that we were cherished.

Grandpa and Grandma Locasio related to each other by bickering. Grandpa was usually the instigator. He and Grandma could be sitting watching the 1960s TV show *Gunsmoke*, and Grandpa would take a big draw from his cigarette and blow it out. He would remark, looking proudly at Hankley his tiny grandson, "When Baby Hankley grows up, he's gonna be King of the Junkyard!"

Grandma would protest, "Now *Inno*, honey, you know that's not true."

She never could stop taking him seriously and he never could stop yanking her chain.

He occasionally antagonized my cousin Natalie, Connie's daughter, in a playful way. When Natalie brought over her doll, Baby Tender Love, to play with at Grandpa and Grandma's house, Grandpa grinned and then said, "You sure do love that Baby Tenderloin."

I can still hear Natalie protesting loudly, "Not TEN-DAH-LOIN! TEN-DAH-LOVE!"

Grandpa would smile and nod. "Yeah, she's real cute. Little Baby Tenderloin."

Nobody but Grandpa could be so good-hearted and such a devil at the same time.

22

GRANDPA AND GRANDMA'S HOUSE, FULL OF BICKERING

Grandpa and Grandma had a 1950s-style Formica-topped table edged with stainless steel, and sand-colored shiny vinyl chairs in their kitchen. The chairs had curvy backs and stainless steel legs. There was a high stool, white with black speckles, in the corner by the sink. During the summer, whenever I sat on one of those vinyl chairs, my leg sweat would cause me to stick to the chair. When I got up, I felt a sting and heard a sound like a Band-Aid being ripped off. I usually sat next to the "high-tech" toaster, which made up to four pieces of toast at a time. I did not have to push a toaster handle like I did at Grandma and Grandpa Miller's house. The toaster sensed the weight of bread and dunked it automatically. I enjoyed inserting the slices of white Wonder Bread and watching the toaster take them down. It didn't take much to please me in those days.

Grandma was meticulous about her appearance. Before going out, she always had her face made up and dressed herself up in a freshly ironed blouse, matching slacks, and high heels. She checked the correctness of her lipstick in the small mirror that hung over the kitchen sink, there specifically for this purpose. Grandma always "dressed to the nines," even to go to Kroger's. She said she never knew who she might meet there.

Grandpa could not care less how he looked. He never minded looking silly. He often sat up straight and told us, "In this house, I'm the king." His diminutive height made him look like a feisty bantam rooster.

He would add, "And I'm smart. I use my head for something other than a hat rack."

One day, Grandma, irritated by his strutting, tried to take him down a notch or two with her sarcasm, "Oh yes, dear. You're so smart. Such brains!"

Then the bickering began. I once sat in their kitchen with a notebook and began transcribing the conversation my grandparents were having:

"Well, I don't know about that. Violet, it sure ain't smart for us to be payin' so much money for that new house we're buyin'. I'm diggin' in my pockets to *donate* to that realtor."

"Inno, I don't want to hear another word about real estate. I'm sick of it. Why don't you find somethin' to do, honey? You just sit on that couch sleepin'!"

"I can't work anymore, Violet. Too old."

"Good heavens, honey, you're not too old. Lots of people older than you are still working. How old do you think Lawrence Welk is?"

"He's makin' a mint of money, that's why he's still workin'."

"He's much older than you are, dear. And he had to start in a small way too. You know, another thing you should have kept up is the clarinet." (She mentioned this even though Grandpa hadn't played the clarinet in 40 years).

"Nah, I can't do that," Grandpa said. He lifted his fingers to his mouth and mimicked a bad clarinet player. "Phee...phee...phee! Heh, heh, heh! All I ever did with my clarinet was play in the City Band!"

"That's 'cos you quit."

"You made me quit!"

"Oh, sure I did, honey. I just love hearin' about all the terrible things I made you do."

At this point, the bickering sped up so much I could no longer keep pace with writing it down. Grandpa finally wandered off to the couch to take a nap, worn out from this energetic exchange.

Later, once rested, he started up again. He took it into his head to make fun of both God and Country, two ways to rile up my most proper grandmother, who revered both, as any good lady of that era did. "Violet! Here's a grace we can say over your chicken at dinner tonight. Bless the Meat, To Heck with the Skin, Open Your Mouth, And Poke It In!"

My grandmother was horrified.

Then Grandpa twinkled, "Kids, I got a new way to sing the National Anthem!" I listened with interest as Grandpa sang in his raspy smoker's voice to the tune of the *Star-Spangled Banner*, "Oh say can you see, any bedbugs on me? If you can, take a few! Then we'll all have some too!"

Grandma was appalled and spit out, "Oh, *Grandpa!*"

As my father often noted, "It doesn't take anything for my mother to have a conniption." (A *conniption* was a fit out of all proportion to the situation. That was how they said it in southern Indiana in those days).

Grandpa had a baseball-oriented song too. He once sang to us:

One night in bed a-sleepin', I heard an umpire call.
The cooties and the bedbugs, played baseball on my wall.
The score was three to nothing, the cooties were ahead.
The bedbugs knocked a home run, and knocked me out of
bed.

Grandpa loved to play and hated to work. Most people have tendencies that way, but Grandpa took it to extremes. Grandma would get on his case about cutting the grass after it got so long it needed a scythe. Grandpa would groan, "I hate rain. It makes the grass grow." But eventually it became unavoidable to do something about it. Grandpa would get out the lawn mower and push it up and down with all his might to get it over with quickly. He had a mutinous scowl on his face the whole time. Dad used to say that Grandpa mowed the yard "like he was killing snakes."

Grandpa worked hard when he had to, but in some ways he was a little boy who never grew up. No wonder he loved having grandchildren. It meant lots of playtime. In the days of the Great Depression, to save water, many people only took baths once a week. Grandpa never got over hating his "Saturday bath." When he married Grandma, she took over right where his mother had left off, sending him upstairs to attend to the weekly hygiene ritual. Grandpa used to run water for a few minutes and then wet his towel and come back downstairs. I wonder how he smelled in those days.

Grandpa could be as stubborn as a little boy too. During the 1930s the stone mill closed. Grandpa lost his job as a stonecutter. He was offered a job taking tickets at the local movie theater. He turned it down saying he wasn't a ticket holder, he was a stonecutter. Grandma had to take a job cleaning rich people's houses. It's amazing that their marriage lasted, but in those days women did what they had to do to survive and that usually meant sticking with their husbands.

Grandpa might have been a stubborn man and a gambling addict, but he was still attached to his mother, Great-grandma Miletti who always had a little money saved up. She also owned their house and made sure my father and his sister had decent clothes for school.

Lisa's dog, Charlie, often stayed with our grandparents and Grandpa was the one who would walk him. Grandpa liked dogs. "Come on, Charlie," he would say early in the morning, "I'll give you a long walk. We don't want one of them two-sprinkle walks. I'm gonna walk you long enough to have twenty-five sprinkles and a big turd. Come on, Charlie, let's go take a big shit!"

This caused Grandma to have another conniption. "Inno, you're too old to talk that way!" Most people tell children they're too young to swear. Grandma thought Grandpa was too old.

I used to love the TV show *The Beverly Hillbillies*, but I never realized that I was living in a family who could have been hillbillies; all they lacked were hills. Some of their relatives, the ones Grandpa used to disparage to irk Grandma, had outhouses at one time, complete with the Sears Roebuck catalog inside...which was good for 650 uses. One time, my great-aunt Josie, Grandma Locasio's aunt, was out driving. She was later taken to task for not greeting her neighbor who was driving by on the other side of the road. Aunt Josie exclaimed, "If I'd-a knowed that was you, I'd-a rech out and wove."

Aunt Josie later went to the dime store in downtown Upperville to buy some handkerchiefs. There were no prices on them so she asked the store clerk how much they were. The young woman quoted a figure that seemed far too high for Aunt Josie, and she said they weren't worth that much. The young lady disagreed. "Miss Josie, Them's Hand-Did!"

Years later, my father called Aunt Josie on the phone, but got his Great-Uncle Horace instead. He was surprised. He thought Horace would be at work and Josie at home. But Horace had a cold that day. Dad noticed that Horace sounded a little stuffy and wasn't sure if it was Horace or the phone that was the problem. He thought he might have called Horace at work by mistake. "Uncle Horace! Where are you?" Dad asked.

Horace drawled, "At the other end of the li-i-i-ne."

There was no way Grandpa could say to Grandma, "I'm feeling lonely and I want to talk." He was endlessly gregarious, which sometimes taxed my quieter grandmother. They might be sitting together watching TV, with Grandma enjoying a few moments of peace without Grandpa's chatter. But Grandpa could not be quiet for long. And he had an unfailing way of getting Grandma to connect with him. Out of a silence, which for him was going on too long, he said, casually, "Violet, that no-good brother of yours never did pay back the ten dollars he owes me."

Grandma was sensitive about her relatives, and this inevitably caused a reaction, meaning screaming at each other. If it wasn't her brother's mooching, it was the fact that her sisters were too fat. Grandpa knew, with cunning accuracy from years of practice, which strings to pull.

In those days, there was no such thing as marital counseling, and my grandparents would not have sought it even if there were, and if they could have afforded it. People who grew up in the Great Depression, with its ethos of self-sufficiency, did not air their dirty laundry to outsiders. It simply wasn't done. Still, something worked. They bickered their way through 53 years of marriage. When Grandpa died, Grandma felt utterly desolate.

Underneath it all, Grandpa adored his wife. On their fiftieth wedding anniversary, he got her a huge, beautiful pink orchid corsage. During the cake cutting at their party at the Loyal Fraternal Order of the Moose Lodge, one of the crowd folk present complimented Grandma on her orchid.

Grandpa lowered his eyes. "Yeah, I cashed the last of my food stamps gettin' that."

Grandma whirled around at him, aghast. "Don't say that! They don't know us that well!" She was drowned out by the howls of laughter from those who knew Grandpa quite well enough.

23

WHAT SPAWNED GRANDPA LOCASIO?

Growing up into a character was Grandpa's destiny. A detour into family history reveals this truth. My grandfather Inno Locasio was the youngest son of our great-grandma Miletti, about whom the Locasio family told endless stories. Grandma Miletti was the stuff of legend. She arrived at Ellis Island with other immigrants on a ship from Sicily. I barely knew her. What I remember about her comes from our very first home leave to America from Wales in 1963. By then, she was close to a hundred years old. With her hooked nose and shrieking, Italian-accented broken English she would yell, "Come to your Grrrrandma MILETTI!"

I would hide behind the sofa. I was terrified of her. I thought she was a witch. In fact, she looked just like the witch in my *Hansel and Gretel* book.

But after Grandma Miletti passed away, I loved hearing the stories about her that Grandpa Locasio and others told me. The main thing I recalled about both Grandpa Locasio and his mother was that both of them were incapable of embarrassment. Others might be embarrassed by their antics, but they said and did exactly what occurred to them, no matter what.

When my father was dating my mother, and trying to impress her, the two of them were walking with Grandma Miletti one cloudy Sunday morning. Grandma, always a good Catholic, was on her way to church for Mass. She carried an umbrella in case it rained. Suddenly, right in the middle of the sidewalk, the elastic on her bloomers snapped and they fell down around her ankles. Grandma neatly stepped out of them and used her other leg to kick those bloomers into her umbrella, which she held half open for the catch. She snapped the umbrella shut and kept walking without missing a step.

Another time when my father and mother were still dating, she invited both of them to come and meet one of her friends. "Come and meet this pully girl," she urged them. Grandma's English was never good and "pully" meant "pretty." My father and mother accepted the invitation and went with Grandma to visit her "pully" friend. However, the woman was not pretty in any sense of the word. She had dishwater-blond, messy hair and crooked teeth. After the visit, my father said, "Grandma, it was nice to meet your friend. But I wouldn't call her pretty."

Grandma threw back her head and cackled with laughter. "Ha-ha-ha! Grandma make a joke! She no pully! Face like horse-a pile!"

When Grandpa and Grandma Locasio first bought their house in Upperville, Great-Grandma Miletti lived with them. (She was called "Grandma" by all generations of her family). This caused some marital conflicts, so Grandpa and Grandma Locasio remodeled the house so that Grandma Miletti had a separate apartment. My grandparents, Inno and Violet, were pleased with this arrangement. Grandma Miletti was not pleased at all. My parents went to visit her in her apartment soon after she had moved into it. She wept aloud that her family had shut her out and cut her off by moving her there. "Is so terrible!" she moaned. "Now, I have no family!" Just then, the upstairs toilet flushed. Grandma emitted a loud dramatic sob. "And they even shit on me!"

Grandma Miletti had no qualms about bragging. When a friend was showing pictures of her two adorable grandchildren to Grandma and a few other women, Grandma nodded, again using the word "pully" to mean "pretty." "They pully, sure. But not as pully as my Ann Lee and Lisa!" She was as unabashed about her Italian cooking. "Mrs. Pizzano makes-a good ravioli. But she-a no make it good like mine!"

My Aunt Rose, Grandma Miletti's granddaughter, reported that Grandma Miletti was "the most immodest woman who ever lived." She had good reasons to make this statement. For example, one summer day after she retired from her housecleaning job, she was home in her apartment, expecting the mailman to deliver some important mail. She had just gotten up and was dressing when she heard some noises outside. She became curious, and decided to see if that was her mail arriving. She hurriedly pulled on a blue cotton dress and went to open the door. It was a plumber who had accidentally come to the wrong house. What the astonished plumber saw was little hook-nosed, wrinkled Grandma Miletti in a disheveled blue dress with one breast hanging out. Grandma Miletti took it all in stride. All she said in her broken English was, "Oh, excuse me. I thought-a you were the mailman!"

Grandma was known all over town for attending every funeral she could. She showed up whether she knew the deceased person or not. She did this for two reasons: She loved socializing with everyone after the service, and she loved to cry. When the clergyman commended the dead stranger's spirit to God, Grandma wailed louder than anyone. The family was appreciative, and Grandma made new friends. She usually got invited to the meal afterwards, which may have been part of the plan.

By the year 1965, Grandma Miletti had died. Nobody knew exactly how old she was. Her birth certificate, if she ever had one, was in Sicily and her papers from Ellis Island were long lost. The family's best guess is that she was almost a hundred years old. But she never saw herself as old. Well into her eighties she talked about how she loved to visit "the old people." They were all younger than she was. She had three husbands. The first husband fathered her first two sons, Luigi and Georgio. Her second husband, Angelo, sired my Grandfather Innocenzio. Angelo was an electrician who died young after touching a live wire. Grandpa Locasio never knew him. After he died, Grandma married the man named Miletti about whom I know nothing.

But I had the joy of knowing Grandma Miletti's youngest offspring, my grandfather. Grandpa Locasio, according to my dad, was an atrocious father. In his younger days, he was addicted to gambling and would disappear after work to the Loyal Order of the Moose Lodge to play poker with his wife's grocery money. I heard stories from my father about his mother storming off to the Moose Lodge and upending poker tables, scattering cards and plastic chips everywhere.

Inno and Violet married at the age of seventeen, and despite their poverty, their stormy marriage, the Great Depression of the 1930s, and World War II, they stayed married until Grandpa died aged 72. My father recalled his father beating him with a belt. When my father got older, he was finally able to outrun his father and the belt. He told tales of his roaring father, bellowing epithets, pursuing him up and down streets all over town.

24

MORE GLORIOUS GRANDPA DAYS

The miracle was that Grandpa Locasio was a much better grandfather than he was a father. Perhaps age and experience mellowed him. He reveled in those trips to Hegg's Drugstore with us and with our cousins, Connie, Babs, and Mark. These cousins were the children of my Aunt Rose and Uncle Jack. I loved them and thought they were cool. They were my only aunt and uncle. Aunt Rose was a much more laid back mother than my own mother. If her children did not like the food she served for a family dinner, she would make them a sandwich. My parents thought this was appalling. I thought it was wonderful, and felt cheated.

Grandpa had my three cousins and us three Locasio kids: six grandchildren to spoil. In addition to those summer trips to Hegg's for toys, he took us to Bryant Park where there were swings, slides, a roundabout, and climbing bars. Most of this equipment has been replaced with plastic play scapes, but Bryant Park's metallic playground equipment worked fine for us. None of us wore safety helmets as we climbed the steps to the top of the towering slide, swung on the steel swings, swirled on the fast-spinning roundabout, or rocketed up and down on the seesaws. Good times.

After swinging, sliding, spinning, and buying toys, Grandpa took us to the Penguin for ice cream. In those days the Dairy Queen was only one option for ice cream and not even the best one. The owner of the Penguin was a personal friend of Grandpa's. Almost everyone in Upperville was a personal friend of Grandpa's. He never knew a stranger. He had multitudes of friends at the Moose Lodge where he had finally gotten his gambling under control. Almost everyone at the stone mill where he worked liked him. He shared his cigarettes, told and heard jokes, and played poker in later years in moderation. Upperville was a fairly small town in those days and Grandpa was greeted everywhere he went. His five feet six inches of height, his thinning white hair, Roman nose, black framed glasses, and green Italian eyes were well known in the town. He wore white cotton shirts and brown polyester slacks. People waved wherever he went.

When I became a teenager, my appreciation for Grandpa lessened. With the self-consciousness of adolescence, Grandpa's ebullience began to embarrass me. I outgrew the playground trips and the paper dolls from Hegg's Drugs, and a dollar of his "blow money" wasn't such a big deal any more.

Once, when I was applying makeup in the living room, experimenting with a shade of plum sparkling lip-gloss, he remarked with the same line, "Even manure would look good on your lips." I snorted. As the sophisticated thirteen-year-old that I was, it was far beneath my dignity to consider kissing a horse pile. His remark no longer was funny to me.

Grandpa had one quirk in his personality that I inherited. He had no sense of direction. Upperville was not difficult to navigate, but my grandfather was directionally dyslexic. He never knew which way to turn. He got where he was going by taking every wrong road possible first. When he finally turned around to come home, he arrived there more or less by accident. He was a safe driver most of the time, but he got distracted easily. "Look, there's Billy Fox!" he would exclaim, rolling down the window to wave at Billy and missing yet another turn. When we were with him, we would go home via the Upperville city limits, heading out into countryside. Grandpa had a singsong refrain. "Grandpa went the WRONG way, but Grandpa found the RIGHT way!" He would turn the car around and try again, crisscrossing Upperville, waving frequently at friends on all the side streets we were discovering along the way.

We didn't mind. Time with Grandpa was time well spent. We had toys, candy, and conversation to distract us. When we got home, my grandmother would sometimes ask Grandpa what took him so long, but as the years went by she stopped asking. She knew the answer. As a more sensitive person than Grandpa was, I used to get horribly embarrassed by missing simple directions like he did. But today, I simply tell everyone that I have "directional dyslexia" and that it is a disability. That earns me sympathy instead of scorn. And it is true. The dyslexic person turn letters around and writes them backwards. I turn directions around and go right instead of left. I have no internal compass. I thank God, the Great Spirit, and my Higher Power every day for whoever invented GPS. It has saved me much misery.

Years later in 1979, my father bought his dream car, an Oldsmobile '98 Regency. It contained a built-in CB radio, my father's glorious new toy. This was one of the years where CB radios were a fad, and not only truckers, but everyone else, seemed to use them. Dad loved the car and the radio so much that when he got home from driving on the I-71 freeway from Cleveland to Strongsville, he would sometimes sit in his driveway and pretend he was still driving, talking to the truckers on the freeway nearby. "Breaker One-Nine, Breaker One-Nine, can I get an eastbound Seven-One?" he requested. There was a buzz of static and then a growly trucker's voice responded. "That guy must be on pills. I-71 runs north and south!"

25

COUSIN MARK

Home visits in the USA during childhood also meant time to play with my cousin Mark. His sisters Connie and Babs were several years older than Lisa and me, so I saw less of the two girls. Mark, however, who was two years older than us, was delighted by our presence. He was the youngest child and the only boy in the family, and he often got pummeled by his older sisters. With us he was the boss. He was sometimes a hard playmate because he was very fast and strong, but usually we had fun. Playing dodge ball with him was rough. He could throw a ball hard enough to sting. And he could easily outrun us back to home base during Hide and Go Seek. He also rigged One Potato, Two Potato, Three Potato, Four so that he was never "It." I didn't figure this out until years later. He was the big kid, the quick kid, the clever kid, and the glamorous kid. The older kid. He outranked me in every way. I was in awe of him.

When Mark taught us to Hide and Go Seek, the bus seat attached to the Williams' oak tree next door was home base. We learned from Mark that when one of us was "It" we must leave home base and actively seek those who were hidden. If we stayed too close to the bus seat, Mark would yell from his hiding place, "Base Hog!" which implied cowardice. Going out and actively seeking others taught me the value of being enterprising. I learned from Mark that however hard it might be, one must go forth into the world and at least pretend to have courage.

When we were teenagers, we visited Aunt Rose and Uncle Jack in Lafayette. Mark was recovering from mononucleosis. We knew well that this was known as "the kissing disease" and I was sure that Mark had contracted it because he had kissed so many girls. To this day, I think I was right. Mark was a handsome and wildly popular young man, in part because he played football, but also because he was good-looking as well as good-natured. Well, most of the time.

He gave me no end of grief because I loved the singer Donny Osmond and all the bubble gum rock of that era, for which he had nothing but disdain. Still, I was genuinely sorry that he had had mono shortly before we went to see him. Fortunately, he was better by then and well enough to haul all our suitcases into the house. I was impressed. I told his mother, my Aunt Rose, "The way Mark carried all those heavy suitcases inside, I can hardly believe he was recently a mononucleosis victim!"

Aunt Rose cracked up laughing. "The way you said that, it sounds like he went through a major natural disaster!"

Mark broke the heart of at least one girl in his class. Her name was Cindy. She wanted to marry him, but it wasn't to be. When Mark married his wife Jane, Cindy came to the ceremony and cried through the whole thing. Some were surprised at his choice of Jane. Nobody predicted Mark winding up with any woman who wasn't a beauty queen. She wasn't considered one of the beauty queens he usually dated. She was almost, as the cliché goes, a "plain Jane." But she challenged him by never taking him too seriously. She still does that today.

When I was ten years old, Grandma Locasio loaned us her reel-to-reel tape recorder and told us we could play with it all afternoon. Mark announced that we would hold a beauty contest. As Mark was the oldest he was the boss, so that's what we did. Mark was the emcee, declaring himself to be Walter Cronkite of the CBS Studios. I never heard of Walter Cronkite emceeing a beauty contest. In real life, Cronkite stuck to being the ultimate evening newsman of the 1960s, but as I said, Mark was the boss. "You have to have fake names," he insisted. "Lisa can be Miss Tapwater, Ann Lee can be Miss Toiletwater, and Angel can be Miss Springwater. I didn't particularly like my name, but what Mark said was law.

He started asking us complex questions such as, "What's your favorite color?" Mark's other questions were similarly inspiring. "What's your favorite game?" He was possibly disappointed when none of us said football. He made other questions up on the fly. Then he suddenly announced, "We'll be right back! Technical Difficulties!" This happened all the time in real life with 1960s TV, so he was imitating what he knew. After he switched off the tape recorder to simulate the technical issues, he told us, "When I turn on the tape recorder, I'm going to ask you, "What do you think of Communism?" You need to say, "*Blecch!*"

Of course we did. We all competed to see who could say "*Blecch!*" the loudest. Mark finally got tired of all the *blecch*-ing and announced another break for technical difficulties. Then he told us to shut up. This question was my first lesson in systems of government, handed to me through Mark. He had heard it from his dad, my Uncle Jack.

Mark had assured us prior to the contest that although he might ask us silly questions, he would choose the winner based on who did the best. All of us fervently hoped that we would get picked. To win Mark's highest award for beauty would be a prize indeed. It was also good training for junior high, where boys who thought you were cute was the biggest affirmation in the world. At the end of the beauty contest, meaning when Mark had had enough and wanted to go play football, he announced the winner.

Miss Springwater got several thousand votes, Miss Tapwater a few thousand more, and Miss Toiletwater got fifty thousand. I was crowned *Miss Beautiful Toiletwater.* I smiled radiantly as Mark placed the paper crown on my head, made out of stuck-together pieces of the spiral notebook paper that Grandma used for her grocery list. It was the happiest day of my whole vacation.

Lisa glared at me as she always did when I received any kind of honor. And Mark went to find Jimmy Williams and practice throwing touchdown passes.

26

MORE MARVELS FROM MARK

In those days, when Mark was young but still older than me (for some reason that never changed) Grandpa and Grandma's house had a backyard that led to railroad tracks. The yard was not fenced. They shared it with their next door neighbor, Mrs. Williams. She was Angel's grandmother and mother to Angel's uncle Jimmy, the boy with whom Mark practiced his football skills. Angel was our playmate and Jimmy was Mark's.

Jimmy was 13 and quiet to the point of being antisocial. He had no interest in our games. All I remember about Jimmy was him saying, "Angel, quit that!" And I also remember that he was fascinated by cars. He had an old Ford in the backyard and would rev up its engine every morning at 6:00 a.m., waking us all next door. I heard the engine whining more often than I heard Jimmy speak.

Whenever I went to see Angel, Jimmy would be sitting watching their black and white TV in loose, oil-stained brown pants and an undershirt. He never greeted us. He pursed his thick lips and looked sulky, as if our showing up had ruined his day. He talked to Mark, though, because of their shared passion for cars. Mark, helped along by Jimmy, could wax eloquent about a tire's PSI and an engine's RPMs in a way that made me admire him all the more.

Mark and Jimmy hung out and worked on Jimmy's car. I never recall seeing it move. It was perpetually up on blocks, (like something out of a Jeff

Foxworthy's redneck joke). A muffler, an air filter, hubcaps, and assorted screws and wrenches littered the landscape outside Jimmy's yard. He had a beat-up, rusty toolbox full of beat-up, rusty tools. The car was fairly beat-up and rusty itself. It fit the scene perfectly for a car-mad town.

Upperville isn't that far from Speedway, which was (and is) where the Indianapolis 500 runs every year on Memorial Day weekend. Just about every red-blooded man in the area, when he wasn't thinking about basketball, football, or politics was talking cars. My two female cousins, as well as Mark, played car songs on Grandpa and Grandma's stereo. "Little Deuce Coupe," "Drive My Car," "GTO," "I Get Around," and other songs regularly blared from our grandparents' living room.

Men and boys debated the carburetors, horsepower of Fords versus Chevys, and Pontiacs versus Buicks versus Cadillacs. The Cadillac was the gold standard, except when the man preferred sports cars, which had their own mystique. One of my relatives became an inspired, crackerjack IBM salesman for the sole reason of wanting to drive Corvettes.

These guys were their cars and their cars were them. They called both their cars and their wives "baby." The marriage could go wrong, however. What stymied them was when they would try to start a car, give it too much gas, and then the aroma of fuel would permeate the air. They would say in utter helplessness, "It's flooded." These days I never hear about a car being "flooded" so presumably a mechanical intervention has prevailed to prevent that from happening.

Mark was all boy as a kid and retained a degree of insolence as an adult. He had a ferocious temper when he was young and once kicked the screen of my grandparents' brand new RCA color console television. That was too much even for the indulgent Grandpa Locasio, making Cousin Mark the only grandchild that Grandpa ever spanked. Mark mellowed when he got older, though. When his own son, Mark Lee, lost his temper with his father at a young age and told Mark, "You're stupid!" Mark didn't say much. Time passed. When Mark Lee had a mechanical problem with his bicycle, he asked, "Dad, can you help me fix my bike?"

Mark shrugged. "I don't know how. I'm stupid!"

Whenever we played cards in Upperville in the 1990s, when Grandma Locasio was still alive, Mark and his wife Jane would come down to join us. It was the custom in our family to designate the two opposing teams "We" and "They." My father was keeping score, so his team was "We." Under the "We" column were a long column of numbers. Under "They" the numbers were sparse. Someone yelled over from the living room, "Who's winning?"

Mark grinned. "We are. WE are ahead. THEY are behind. However, *They* are *We* and *We* are *They.*"

When he wasn't playing cards, Mark loved to fish. Grandpa Locasio taught him. He used to take little Mark to local creeks and limestone quarry holes in Upperville when Mark was young. Mark caught the fishing bug. He still goes on an angling trip each year with his buddies to a place called Bear Island. At least that was its official name. One year, they were gathered at their cabin and after refrigerating the day's catch, they shot a video of all ten men mooning the camera. Mark's voice-over explained, "That's why they call it Bare Island."

Mark is now 59 with scant gray hair, glasses, and usually a cigarette between his fingers. He looks like the grandfather he is. He still owns and runs the biggest tire and auto repair shop in the area and is respected as the most honest mechanic in town. Twenty years ago, he did half a million dollars worth of business. I know this because Uncle Jack liked to brag on his son. These days he probably rakes in much more.

Honest mechanics are hard to come by. He claims to remember nothing of rigging One Potato, Two Potato, Three Potato, Four in his favor. He still owes me for that.

27

AN ANGEL WHO WASN'T

W hen Mark and his sisters departed from Grandpa and Grandma
Locasio's house to visit their other grandparents, Lisa and Angel
and I played other games. Jimmy, of course, ignored us as always. Angel
looked angelic and spent her whole life contradicting the name. She was
a lovely child with soft curly brown hair and long eyelashes adorning her
blue eyes. And she was wilder than a joker in a poker game. It was during
a later home leave in 1967 (our home leaves to the USA were always in
odd-numbered years) that Angel started a fire in the garage. For some odd
reason, my grandmother objected to this situation.

On the other side of my grandparents' house from the Williams
home was an empty lot. Angel and Lisa and I used to pretend we lived
there with no parents; we had a wild and carefree life, and survived by
hunting and fishing. Best of all, in our imaginary world, nobody had to
go to school. The grassy lot on which we played had neither fish nor wild
animals on it, but our imaginations took care of that. We created our own
little world on that plot of tall grass with its dandelions and scattered sticks.
We "went hunting" with our "bows and arrows," as we shot sticks from rubber bands to kill the wild animals roaming in that vacant lot on East Ninth
Street. We shot deer and cooked them over an imaginary fire, just like the
American Indians did. We hid from our enemies who were crouched behind
the weeds. Those weeds were almost tall enough to hide someone our size.

On another occasion, Angel was very upset with her Grandma Williams about something that lady had done. Most likely Angel's grandma had punished her for some misdeed, (Angel was forever committing misdeeds). But that day, Angel said she had had enough and was running away from home. Naturally, we were thrilled. We pictured Angel journeying into the wild blue yonder inside one of the open freight cars that always stood on the railroad tracks. Who knew where she might end up? What adventures she would have!

She came to say goodbye to us with her small suitcase. I asked her what was in it and she opened it. It contained her pajamas and a teddy bear. Angel wasn't overly experienced in packing for long trips. A friend of her Uncle Jimmy's talked her out of running away. I was terribly disappointed. That was a pattern. Angel would propose a plan that to me sounded thrilling and daring, but a person with a voice of reason would step in and scrap the idea. Still, they were exciting while they lasted.

Angel managed to get her grandmother back, though. When I was ten years old, and our family was going back to England soon after our American vacation, Grandma Locasio again let us have her reel-to-reel tape recorder so that Lisa and I and Angel could tape a conversation. Angel thought this was wonderful as her grandmother did not have one. However, when faced with the microphone for the first time, she became nervous and could not think of anything to say. Several times she said, "Goodbye, Annalee and Lisa" (she always called me Annalee for some reason). "I'm real sorry to see you go and I hope you come back soon."

I chimed in with "Thank you, ANGEL!"

Then once again Angel would be offered the microphone. "Goodbye, Annalee and Lisa, I'm real sorry to see you go..." she repeated.

"Thank you, ANGEL!" I said, again.

Finally Lisa got tired of the repetition and said, "Angel, say something else."

Angel thought about it for a moment and then said, "Well, okay. One day my Ma-maw was scrubbin' the floor down at our farm, and she backed up against the door, and there was a great big wasp there, and it stung her right in the bottom. And she was *a'screamin'*, and the whole house came *a'runnin'*, and after we put somethin' on it, we just laughed at her."

Poor Mrs. Williams finally heard the tape after it had been played at not one but two family gatherings, which we held prior to our departure. I wonder how she felt, knowing that having her butt stung by a wasp was common knowledge not only to her next door neighbors, but to all her neighbors' relatives.

Angel taught me two great insults to use in my preteen years. In junior high, she was having her usual verbal battles with her arch enemy, Mark Levine. In the midst of a quarrel Angel yelled at Mark, "I hate you!"

Mark retorted, "Tough shit!"

Angel shot back, "Chew harder!"

Mark told Angel, "Go to hell!"

Angel answered, "I have! Your mother's fine!"

28

MAGICAL TIMES WITH THE MILLERS

My other set of grandparents, Grandpa and Grandma Miller, were just as devoted to us as our paternal grandparents. We were their only grandchildren. Unlike Grandma Locasio, Grandma Miller was extremely active in her community of Normalville. She enjoyed her local sorority, Zeta Beta. (Zeta Beta's secret farewell: "Zeta Beta: See Ya Later!") She was a Girl Scout leader for many years. Grandma was also active in the Normalville Methodist Church. She was a member of the young woman's "Tri Mu" Sunday school class, which stayed together for enough years to become a very old woman's Sunday school class. "Tri Mu" or Three-M in Greek letters, stood for Mind, Morals, and Missions. That group of women was bonded like glue.

Grandpa and Grandma Miller had to cope with adversity, so the Sunday school class provided support for her. In the 1920s, Grandpa Miller suffered his leg injury. In those days there was no Worker's Compensation. He gave up being a mechanic and ran the town's tavern, and later the small grocery store. In 1963, he had another health crisis, suffering a serious attack of spinal meningitis. He almost died. He said later how he knew, struggling for his life in a hospital bed, that his wife as well as the whole Methodist Church was praying for him. He came close to death and that led to a conversion experience. He never put it like that. Grandpa wasn't one to talk about his feelings. But he made promises to God about abstinence from alcohol and promised regular worship; he kept his word. Whatever his faults, Grandpa was a man who kept promises. Being a man of relatively few words, he never said aloud that he was grateful for his life being spared, but his never missing church said it all. And despite being crippled, he lived into his early eighties. The meningitis had weakened him so he was not able to keep up with running a grocery store. He turned to a new livelihood, which would sustain him for the rest of his days.

He turned his garage into a carpenter's shop and started making beautiful wooden toys. That was when I was old enough to really know him. I have only a vague recollection of him in his grocery store. I can still clearly see in my mind's eye the Millers' garage, which contained shelves, hand tools for woodworking, and rows of toys. He had an electric saw and a sander, both of which generated piles of sawdust that covered the floor.

There were varnished, unpainted wooden fire trucks with sturdy removable ladders. Grandpa also made tow trucks with cable and metal hooks. A child could hook and raise another toy vehicle for towing. He made doll-sized chests of drawers. The drawers pulled out and could be removed, and the dressers had mirrors on top of them. Wooden wardrobes with tiny doors on gold hinges matched the dressers. The toys were sturdy enough to be passed down from generation to generation because they were so carefully made. Grandma Miller noted, "There's nothing to wear out about them." My crippled grandfather was a meticulous craftsman. Grandpa Miller always had more orders for toys than he could fill. People were content to wait for months to get their toys. Grandma often chided Grandpa for not charging more for them. Grandpa would respond in his typical hillbilly way, "A feller can charge hisself out of business."

Before he became crippled, Grandpa crafted bigger furniture out of wood. Woodworking was always his hobby, even before it became his livelihood. A floor-to-ceiling hutch, which held the Millers' best china, was his creation. So were two wooden lamp bases with inlaid carvings of flowers. I still have those two lamps, a tall one and a shorter one. As Grandpa was fond of saying, "I always did like to monkey around with wood."

My recollections of visits to the Miller grandparents were of watching Grandpa "monkey around" with his wide variety of machines and his halting walk with that cane. I can still picture him in his green plaid shirts with front pockets and his gray slacks. The slacks had a brown tinge to them because they were always covered with sawdust. Everything in the garage, including Grandpa, was covered with sawdust. At times, he resembled a tan-colored snowman. When I knew him, he was completely bald except for the sawdust covering his bald pate. He always wore those black-framed glasses. He looked like Mr. Potato Head.

At the Miller house, the car was never in the garage. It sat in the driveway, even during the bitterest winters. The garage was for the machines, which were vital for producing toys. Because of his crippled leg, Grandpa could only work for a short while. When his leg started to hurt him, he would sit down in one of the white wooden Adirondack chairs he had made before his leg was injured. The chair sat next to a shelf on which was an old battered off-white radio, always tuned to the local Normalville station that broadcasted baseball games. Grandpa followed those avidly. He would say, "I work awhile, then rest awhile." Today I find that philosophy both simple and profound. Grandpa understood life balance.

As a young child, I would climb into Grandpa's lap while he rested. His cane would be hooked on the back of the chair, and he would usually be chewing tobacco. He always had several empty coffee cans scattered around the garage to catch his spit. I did not like that much, but I liked Grandpa. I would inquisitively ask him, "Are you chewing gum?"

He would reply, "No, it's tabacky. Ya want some?" He grinned and pointed at the round "Mail Pouch Tobacco" metal container in his plaid shirt pocket.

I puckered my lips and said, "Ugh."

Grandpa kept grinning.

We had another joke too. Grandpa had a nickname in high school. He was known as "Enos." I never knew how he got that name or what it meant. But when I was five years old, I would ask him, "What's your name?"

He would answer, "Enos!"

I would make a face. "No it isn't. It's Grandpa Miller."

His face would light up as if he had had a revelation. "Oh! Grandpa Miller! I forgot that!"

I often wondered why Grandpa almost never went to the toilet once he finished his breakfast each morning. He was an early riser, up by 6:00 a.m. and into the garage to start work by seven. Only rarely did he leave his tools and machines to go inside to the bathroom. I found this perplexing. Later I found out from some male relatives, who are my age, that Grandpa had a hole in the ground behind the garage for such purposes. The boys knew about it. Lisa and I did not. It was in a secluded spot covered with a license plate. I smile as I think of the male bonding that probably took place there between Grandpa and the boys. I took that as an explanation as to why people in books never seemed to go to the toilet, but Grandpa was nothing like the characters in the books I read.

I heard later that Grandpa Miller, whose first name was Thomas, was an unusual student and quite a renegade in his youth. I never knew exactly what misbehavior he engaged in, but I did know that school never interested him much. He was incredibly smart, but he only worked at what he liked, so his achievements were uneven. His grades in English were great. He scraped by in history. He liked math and was good at it, which probably went along with his skill in woodworking. He loved shop and carpentry, of course. He was brilliant at Latin. In later years, he put this skill in Latin to use in his garage, working crossword puzzles with ease in his white wooden chair during his rest periods. He could figure out crosswords from all the word derivatives he had learned in Latin class. What he failed in high school, and failed regularly, was "Deportment," an old-fashioned word for good conduct. My Grandpa Miller got a few passing grades, some very good grades, but an F in conduct. I would love to know what he did to get those Fs in Deportment. As one of his friends said, "Thomas Miller *stayed* in trouble."

Grandpa Miller turned some colorful phrases in his speech. When he and Grandma and I went to church, he always headed back to the car immediately after the service. I would go with him. Grandma would linger. When I asked Grandpa where she was, he would sigh. "She's unloadin' her gab."

There was a shiftless and often shirtless fellow named Steve who lived across the backyard, and the back of their house faced the Millers. Steve used to lay out in the summer sun and only move when necessary. He was a constant fixture. Grandpa called him "Cyclone," but I'm not sure why. Maybe it was irony. Cyclone is another word for a tornado, and Steve was most unlike a tornado in his perpetual lack of motion. The same sort of thing happens in small towns when someone with an enormous tomcat calls him "Itty Bitty."

29

MERRYMAKING IN THE MILLERS' BACKYARD

Grandpa never called my mother by her name. Mom told me that he often called her It. "It's coming to see us," he would grin to my grandmother. "It's bringing her kids." He would also call her "the baby." "The baby's visiting her aunt," he told us one day when we arrived home from shopping with Grandma. Perhaps realizing that Mom was now a middle-aged woman, he grinned and added, "But It sure is an old baby!"

When my mechanically-minded brother built up his skills by creating gadgets with Tinker Toy, Legos, and the Erector Set, it was often difficult to discern what purpose he had in mind other than multitudinous gears turning in both directions. While my father often observed that little Hankley had built another "Whing Ding," Grandpa Miller merely said that he had put together a "Manure Grinder."

We had playmates across the Millers' unfenced yard. Their neighbors Bob and Ethel Joiner were the parents, and we loved playing with their daughter Suzy. Suzy was three years older than I was, and she used to come over and play with us on our grandparents' back porch. The back porch became "The Clubhouse" and we drew and colored signs announcing that this was indeed our club. We declared it to be "Girls Only" and told the nearby neighborhood boys Mitch, Mick, and Marty that they could not join. It was fun to be exclusive in those days. And we had the young girls' typical disdain for the opposite sex. They repaid us by standing by the windows and peeking in. To stop them from spying on us, we covered the windows with poster board.

We would sit around the table in the enclosed back porch, draw, paint pictures, and then beg Grandma Miller for some spare change so we could go to the local five-and-dime store to buy candy and cheap toys. The store sold colorful plastic whistles that blew loud enough to cause ringing in the ears. There was an irritable old lady who lived just down the street named Mrs. Martin. We gave her a wide berth as she did not like children. She liked plastic whistles even less. Suzy told us solemnly, "If old Miz Martin hears you blow a whistle, she'll make you eat it."

The store also sold slingshots. We were lucky that we never put anyone's eyes out, caused a concussion, or broke any windows. We loved pulling the strong rubber band on the slingshot back, back, back, aiming it toward the sky, and snapping the band. The rock flew up, up, up. Sometimes we had to take cover so it would not crash-land on one of our heads.

We practiced creative art too. We borrowed some flour from Grandma Miller and mixed it with water to make a white paste. We scooped up some soil and mixed that with water to make a dark brown paste. Then we gathered some ever-abundant sawdust and made it into a light brown paste. We had some large sheets of poster paper on hand and we made some crude pictures with our "paints" out in the driveway. We thought they were wonderful. Then Lisa got the idea that we should try to sell them. So we went up and down East Fillmore Street where my grandparents lived, and tried to get the neighbors to buy our creations. Not surprisingly, they turned us down. One kindly neighbor, old Mrs. Bynum, explained that she had a daughter who painted as well, so she had all the pictures she needed. We were disappointed, but then decided we would be generous and just give them away. We left a picture on everyone's steps.

When we told Grandma what we had done she almost had a conniption fit. "What will the neighbors think?" she gasped. That was pretty much the go-to response in small-town Normalville in those days. One had to stay in good standing with the neighbors, not only because of what they might think, but because of what they might say. One's reputation was a tenuous matter, and Grandma went to great lengths to uphold hers in the community. She was ever mindful that these neighbors were in her church, bridge club, and Zeta Beta sorority. She made us go and pick all those pictures up. By then, the paste had begun to dry. I remember as we carried them back that the crumbling flour, soil, and sawdust got all over our clothes.

Grandpa's wood shop provided a wide scope for creativity. We found an old date stamp, except instead of a date, it had his name on it: Thomas S. Miller. We used it to stamp all our clubhouse "documents" and declared that without the hallowed stamp, nothing could be "official." Old Maxwell House coffee cans, which Grandpa used for tobacco spittle, got commandeered by us before Grandpa could spit in them. We made drums out of them. They were large cans—thrifty Grandma Miller always bought in bulk long before the big box stores—and when we pounded on their plastic lids with a stick or with our hands, we made a satisfactory *thunk thunk*. We banged away on our homemade instruments as we marched way down to the other end of East Fillmore Street from my grandparents' house to where Aunt Alice and Uncle Fred lived. We knocked on the door, and when a surprised Aunt Alice answered, we sang and banged along as follows:

> *Will you let us sing a song, Will you truly let us?*
> *Will you let us play the drum, Will you truly let us?*
> *Will you let us dance for you, Will you truly let us?*
> *Will you let us, is it true? Will you truly let us?*

Aunt Alice, perhaps realizing that we had already assumed permission by singing the song all the way through, just raised her eyebrows and exclaimed, "YES! I will truly let you!"

Looking back, I see the amused twinkle in her eye that belied her sarcastic tone. She then invited us in for some homemade cake and let us sing and bang a while longer. In return, we admired her sizable vegetable garden.

She grew the best green beans, which Grandma Miller always boiled for hours with massive additions of bacon fat. I have never again encountered green beans so divine. Aunt Alice lived to be well past 80 despite the fact that she smoked like a furnace. It may have been the plethora of plants that she and Uncle Fred consumed, straight from her garden.

Uncle Fred smoked, too. He went bald early. I never saw him with hair, other than a dusting of white sprigs scattered over the top of his head like sparse grass in a drought. If Uncle Fred's hair had been wheat, the birds would have had to kneel down to eat it. Fred smoked instead of talking; he never said much to us, although his granddaughter, Cathy, said he talked to her often. They were close. Anytime I saw Fred, he was always to be found in his grey vinyl recliner, reading through his glasses, with a Lucky Strike dangling from his lips. He must have moved around now and then, but I don't remember ever seeing him do it.

He did invent gadgets, though, presumably when I wasn't looking. I saw a spring-lock device he once assembled. "Fred invented that," Alice told us, pointing to it and showing us how it worked. "He never did get a patent for it. I never understood why. Well, lunch is ready. Fred, come to the table! Hurry up, Fred!"

Passive, slow-paced Fred never seemed to get ruffled by Alice's harassment. He sat in his chair and told stories sometimes. He always began by saying to Cathy, "Did I *ever* tell you…? Then he would tell a story he had told many times before.

I am happy for youth today who can text each other day and night, who play on PlayStation and Wii, who have meticulous hand/eye coordination from playing *Halo*, *Game of Thrones*, or whatever video games are popular at the time. I am happy for them. And at the same time, I would not trade the paint we made by watering down flour and mud and sawdust, or the plastic whistles, slingshots, or old Maxwell House coffee cans. Call me crazy, but that's how I feel.

The most fun we ever had at my Miller grandparents' house was the night of the Great Grape Fight. My grandparents had grapevines, but the grapes were sour. I never knew, and never asked, whether they used those grapes in any way. In the summer of 1967, Suzy, Lisa and I challenged Suzy's brothers to a grape fight. The contest was set to begin at dusk. Grandpa had plenty of old empty coffee cans, in which we collected almost every grape on the vine that our opponents had not already picked. We used trash can lids for shields to prepare for the flying grapes that the enemy would be throwing. At dusk, we prepared to battle.

The locusts were brushing their wings together in that unique whirring sound that locusts make in the Midwest, a *"weeeeer, weeeeer, weeeeer."* The lights were on inside the Millers' house as twilight fell and the stars came out, and Grandpa was sitting just inside his lighted garage, on the edge of the driveway, with a crossword puzzle on his lap and a baseball game coming from the radio. It took less than fifteen minutes to throw all the grapes at each other. We declared the fight a draw. Grandpa's vines were picked clean. I wondered if he cared. We never heard anything about it, so probably not. Or else he did not notice, until it was too late, that all his grapes were gone.

But when we loosed a brick free from the top of my grandparents' incinerator, and threw it inside the trash-burning device, he did care about that. Grandpa and Grandma Miller burned their trash in that incinerator, which resembled a three-sided brick fireplace. There were no smoke ordinances in those days. Everybody burned anything flammable in an incinerator. The town was small enough that the smoky smell was not a big problem. I recall the faint smell of smoke in the air, but it was all just part of being in Normalville. But the day Grandpa Miller saw us pick up the brick and drop it into the incinerator, he yelled, "You kids quit throwin' those bricks in there!" I had never heard Grandpa shout that loud or shake his cane that hard. We got that brick out of there and never did it again. It was the one time Grandpa lost his temper with us.

When Grandma finished preparing a meal, she always sent me out to the garage to call Grandpa in. I always did it the same way from the time I was tiny. "Grandpa, come *right now*," I would command him.

"Right now? Well! Okay!" Grandpa would reply and then grin and spit a string of tobacco juice into the Maxwell House can. Then he'd pick up his cane, limp across the garage, and up the steps to the door that separated the kitchen and the garage. Soon we heard the sound of running water in the bathroom as he washed the sawdust off his hands. Then we all sat down to eat. Grandma always asked me to "return thanks," which meant say grace.

After grace, I got to watch Grandpa eat. And hear him too. Nobody had worse table manners than Grandpa. He chewed with his mouth open. We could see everything he ate and the degree to which it had disintegrated between his teeth. He ate with gusto. Chomping and smacking sounds erupted repeatedly from his mouth. Bits of food dropped from his jaws down to the plate. His burps were long and loud. He would let loose with a vibrant "*Aaaauupp!*"

My grandmother, a slender ladylike woman with gray-framed cat's glasses and wavy gray hair, would sometimes wince at her husband's behavior. But I suspect she had long since given up trying to change him. She also rolled her eyes at the trail of sawdust he left everywhere he walked. By the time I came along, Grandma Miller was a patient, long-suffering woman.

I did not know until 2014 that Grandpa Miller had another side. I have since made friends with my cousin Cathy, daughter of Florence Caldwell, my grandfather's sister's child. Cathy told me, "Thomas Miller used to eat goo toast for breakfast. The rest of the day, he went through a case of beer." (Goo toast was white toasted bread with a mixture of peanut butter and corn syrup or molasses mixed together, and then spread on top.)

My mother once mentioned in passing that when she was young, Grandpa hit her across the mouth. I don't know if this happened just once or more often. It doesn't matter. Once would be enough. I do know that my mother rarely talked about her childhood experiences with her parents. She rarely spoke to him even when she was an adult, when we stayed with them during home leave.

Grandpa seemed good-natured enough to me. I didn't know then about the stories and secrets surrounding us.

30

MORE MILLER FAMILY FOLLIES

For relief from her volatile husband, Grandma Miller turned to her wide circle of friends from her sorority, bridge club, and church. While Grandpa Miller was not a big talker, Grandma was highly sociable. When she was not attending a community event, she got together with her three sisters and played bridge for hours. She loved bridge and was good at it. She often made Grand Slams and Small Slams. Being Grandma, she talked of her triumphs endlessly, reveling in victorious memories.

Although a patient and calm woman, Grandma was a steely competitor. She loved to win. And equally she hated to lose. To this day, although I do not play bridge, I can recite the rules I once learned from her. "Fourteen points to open, four to six to answer, ten or eleven to overcall. Lead the card that's fourth from your longest and strongest. If you're going for a Slam, use the Blackwood Convention." Sometimes a person did not have the required number of points in their hand and for that reason had not bid for a long time. Then she might not bid a club confidently but say with an apologetic look, "I'll just *inkle* a club." "Inkling" was fun but risky. One could lose a lot of points that way and end up with a furious partner snapping, "What were you thinking?" Then again, it sometimes worked. Grandma was known to bid on a wing and a prayer and get away with it.

The defining feature of Grandma's life, other than her community good works and its accompanying social life, was how nosey she was.

There is a British slang term for such a person. He or she is called a "Nosey Parker." If they had known my grandmother, it would have been a Nosey Miller. She used to chide us for listening in on her party line, (in those days phone lines were shared among two or more residences). But I caught her doing it, too. "I thought my neighbor might be going to the hospital and if she was, I'd want to help," she explained to me once, quickly hanging up the phone. In the days of party lines, everyone listened in. And she did run the county hospital switchboard for a while. I can only imagine how she must have loved that.

I often helped my grandmother snap and de-string the green beans for supper. "Let's go do them on the front porch," she would urge me.

"Oh Grandma, it's kind of hot out there," I would complain as a child. "And there are flies," I added. Can't we do it in here where it's cool?"

"No," Grandma would counter. "I want to see what all the neighbors are doing. Bob Graham got arrested last week. I want to see if he's home from jail yet." The Grahams were next door neighbors and Grandma kept a close eye on their comings and goings.

She was lucky. With the Grahams next door and the Joiners behind her, she never ran out of things to talk about. So we would have conversations about everyone's deeds and misdeeds, snapping beans all the while into the stainless steel stock pot, rocking on the green wicker rocking chairs. There was a house directly opposite us, but Grandma never talked about the woman who lived there. She must have led an exemplary life. How boring.

Mom spent sizable chunks of time with her extended family, which likewise gave her an escape from her less than wonderful home life. Grandma and Grandpa's sisters, brothers, cousins, uncles, and aunts constantly gathered for potlucks. Grandma's recipe books were well used, covered in gravy and flour stains, from the numerous casseroles and cakes she produced for those occasions. When I visited from Europe, I thought potlucks were thrilling.

They didn't happen in Germany or England, at least not in the posh circles my parents frequented. People had cocktail parties, or met at restaurants, or had fancy dinner parties, but they never held potlucks. To the elegant Booz Allen & Hamilton crowd, a potluck would have been something poor people did, and therefore unthinkable. But I loved them. At the first potluck I remember, at my Aunt Gladys's graceful pillared-entrance farmhouse in Danville, Indiana, I tried watermelon for the first time ever. I thought my mouth was drowning. My sister hated it. She said it, "tasted like a swimming pool."

Not all of the family were popular. Uncle Gilbert was one of the "black sheep." He was my great-uncle by marriage, a farmer, and almost universally considered a horse's rear end except that this would be speaking unkindly of equine anatomy. Uncle Gilbert in his youth persuaded Uncle Ronald, another great-uncle of mine by marriage, to partner with him to buy and later sell a flock of sheep for profit. Uncle Ronald then went off to serve in World War II. When he got back from Europe after the war, Uncle Gilbert told him, "We had some sheep get sick. Half of them died. Your half."

Poor Uncle Ronald. He had it rough all over. When he came back from the war, he opened up a restaurant. Over time, he ran two cafeterias, the one in town, the one in a nearby town, and Ronald's Cafeteria on the bypass when that opened up. Ronald worked 364 days a year, probably to cope with his PTSD. He took off only on Christmas Day, the one day he closed the restaurants.

He showed up at the family gatherings looking odd in civilian clothes instead of his mustard-colored restaurant smock and slacks. He would get drunk as quickly as possible and then pass out on the couch. We tried to have the gift exchange early in the day before Ronald conked out. We also attempted to cheer him up in any way we could. One year, he got a pair of black spandex briefs with the Burger King logo on the front that said, "Home of the Whopper."

My father always joked with him at the family gatherings, because that was the only time he could socialize with Ronald. "Ronald, every time I visit with you, you're taking a day off from work."

AUNT PAULINE AND AUNT GLADYS

T he other "black sheep" in the family was Aunt Pauline, my cousin by marriage. Aunt Pauline was one of the few female motorcycle gang members in those days. They weren't as rough as the Hell's Angels, but still pretty wild. My cousin Harry loved her devil-may-care attitude and found it glamorous. He also relished his parents' despair that he was dating a woman from the notorious Cooper family; everyone in Normalville knew that that family was "trouble." Harry thought Pauline was wonderful. The local hometown Zeta Beta sorority, however, did not. When Pauline's name came up for possible membership, the current members had a ceremony where they anonymously put either a white marble or a black marble in a dark blue cloth drawstring bag, signifying acceptance or rejection. Aunt Pauline was "blackballed." As this rarely happened, it leaked out and caused quite a stir.

Ten years later, my mother and father went to Uncle Harry and Aunt Pauline's house for a Christmas party. Aunt Pauline kept filling and refilling their holiday punch glasses. When my parents got up to go home, they felt the room tilt as if they were on an airline, circling around to align with the runway. When my parents got home they staggered though the front door, holding onto the wall for support. I've never seen my parents that drunk before. And that is saying a lot. My father reviled Aunt Pauline the next morning for her ever-flowing liquor as he nursed a massive hangover. But

113

while he raged over the evil she had done, I couldn't help but think that it wasn't as if Aunt Pauline had done anything that they were not aware of at the time.

Aunt Pauline got drunk herself at a summer family reunion in Evansville in the late 1960s. While intoxicated, she discovered I had gone to the toilet in the upstairs restroom that didn't lock. She walked in, stood against the sink, crossed her legs, folded her arms, and watched me go. "You're slow at that," she observed. "You need to speed up."

Later that day, she brought a cat into the house and kept offering it up at face level to my Great-Aunt Phoebe who had a cat phobia. Aunt Phoebe threatened to clock her one upside the head. Then, Aunt Pauline brought a rabbit into the house and watched the cat chase the rabbit until the rabbit paused on an antique floral rug with cream-colored fringe on it. The bunny let fly with a stream of round black pellets. The hostess was not amused.

Aunt Pauline, although married to Harry, loved to flirt with my father. She often paid him special attention, and as my sister and I grew to be teenagers, we learned to watch for her touching his arm, batting her eyelashes, and laughing loudly at his jokes whether they were funny or not. We loved it. It made my mother livid. Aunt Pauline's actions were bad enough, but our eagerness to witness them made it worse.

To be fair, Aunt Pauline has now cleaned up her act and become a born-again Christian. She attends a mega-church on the outskirts of town. The family in turn has responded kindly and has let bygones be bygones. But sometimes I still miss her making passes at my father, the cats and rabbits playing tag in the house, and all that wild motorcycling. I am thankful, though, that I am safe from unexpected restroom companionship and can use the commode in peace, concentrating on the business at hand.

While Aunt Pauline was wild, Aunt Gladys could be mildly mischievous. We kids all loved Aunt Gladys. She was a magnet for children. With a low-key and gentle manner, she was the family's best listener. I'm glad someone was. Everyone else was a talker. Aunt Gladys would hear my stories, which ranged from the ordinary to the unbelievable, with wide attentive eyes and respond, "Well! Is that right!" When as a young adult I was headed off to a brief stint at Georgetown Law School, Aunt Gladys shook her head in wonder as she always did and said, "I'm glad you've hitched your wagon to a star."

Aunt Gladys had one quirk. She was a secret smoker and believed that her husband, my Uncle Don, did not know about it. When I stayed at their farmhouse, I would pass by the guest bathroom on my way in and see trails of blue smoke wafting through the crack between the closed door and the doorjamb.

When Gladys came out I asked, "Have you been smoking?"

Gladys put her index finger to her lips and gasped, "Ssh! don't let Don hear you!"

Don had been a smoker too, but quit. He now, as is the case with so many former smokers, loathed the smell of smoke and became quite the evangelist for getting others to quit. But he had no success with his wife.

I could smell stale cigarettes all over Aunt Gladys when she emerged from that bathroom. She came out and sprayed air freshener where she had vacated the room. "Do you have a Life Saver?" she asked me. "I need one for my breath. When I see Don, it will save my life!"

After visiting Gladys, I returned to Normalville. Grandma always insisted we go to the Normalville Methodist Church when we visited. She loved showing off her grandchildren who, she secretly knew, were better than anyone else's. She loved to talk about us. Truthfully, Grandma loved to talk about anything. To anyone. At any time.

Whenever I took a candid photo of Grandma in a group, she always had her eyes shut and her mouth wide open…talking.

32

ABOUT AUNT ETOILE: YES, THAT WAS REALLY HER NAME

Grandma's best friend was a woman named Etoile Talley. We called her Aunt Etoile because she was a close friend of our whole family. Her husband, Harold, died when I was young so I never knew him, but I knew Aunt Etoile for two decades. During her working years she was a nurse at the Normalville Hospital. She loved to talk just as much as my grandmother did. She had curly off-white hair, silver-framed cat's glasses, buck teeth, and a plump figure that resulted from loving her own cooking. A mean-spirited person might have called her ugly, but Aunt Etoile was too much fun, too vibrant, and too full of laughter to be thought of in that way. She had a loud, merry voice.

I can still recall going to visit at her farmhouse out in the country. We would knock on the door and would hear, "HELLO-O-O! Come in! Come in!" Whenever we visited, it was as if our arrival were the greatest gift that had ever been bestowed on her.

Aunt Etoile loved to tell dirty jokes. She had an endless supply of them. She said that while she worked with doctors and other nurses, dirty jokes simply flowed. It seemed to have something to do with working with the human body all day. In my younger years, Aunt Etoile tried to be careful about not telling her dirtiest jokes near us. But I quickly found ways to eavesdrop. It was too much fun to miss. I did not always understand the punch lines at first, but I got better at it.

I remember in particular, a story Aunt Etoile told about the young man who was in the hospital with a broken leg. A middle aged nurse gave him a bath and afterwards came to the other nurses and gasped, "That man has 'swan' tattooed on his penis!"

Another middle aged nurse said, "I want to see that. I'll give him his bath tomorrow." So she did. She came out of the man's room and told the others, "It's true. He has 'swan' tattooed on his penis!"

Then, a pretty young nurse said that she, too, wanted to see what the others were talking about. So the following day she gave him a bath. She then came to the other nurses and said, "You're wrong. The word isn't 'swan.' It's 'Saskatchewan!'"

When I posted this story on Facebook, I got accused of ageism. Perhaps that's fair. But Etoile sure made it funny in the telling.

My favorite Etoile joke was the one about the married couple who decided to have a big dinner party. At the last minute, they discovered they had completely run out of toilet paper. This was in the old days, long before 7-11s stood on every corner. The wife was a skilled seamstress, and a quick thinker. She told her husband, "It's all right, I have some old dress patterns in the upstairs closet. We can use those; they're soft and made of tissue. So they got the patterns, folded them neatly, and placed them in the washroom. After dinner, one of the female guests went into the bathroom and came out with a strange look on her face. "Can I speak to you privately?" she requested. As the couple came close, she quietly told them, "I've seen a lot of strange things in my life, but this is the first time I've seen toilet paper marked front and back."

My other favorite joke of Etoile's was the one about the elderly nun teaching first grade at a Catholic school. It was the end of the day and the nun had a few moments before school was dismissed. She started asking the children what they wanted to be when they grew up. Little Mary said she wanted to be a nurse.

"Oh! A nurse! Taking care of the sick! That's doing God's work, Mary. Very good."

Then Freddie put up his hand and said, "I want to be a firefighter."

The nun smiled. "Putting out fires is very important! Very nice, Freddie."

Then Susie raised her hand. "I wanna be a prostitute."

The nun blanched white as a sheet. "Wh-WHAT did you say?"

Susie repeated, "I wanna be a prostitute."

The nun sighed. "Thank heavens, child. I thought you said a Protestant."

Etoile told dirty jokes about Catholics, Jews, Arabs, Presbyterians, and others in those less enlightened days. Nobody escaped. For all of Aunt Etoile's jokes about religion, she would not tolerate us children saying "Oh God!" If we did that, she would wag a finger at us and shake her head. "Don't take the Lord's name in vain, honey," she admonished. With Aunt Etoile, jokes about immoral ministers and drunk nuns were fine, but God had to be respected. It made an odd contrast to some of her stories that, as my Dad put it, were "enough to make your hair curl."

In one of her stories, a young nurse got mixed up. She went into a hospital room with a pan of steaming hot water. A naked male patient ran out of the room screaming, "I thought that nurse came in to prick my boil!"

Etoile either started or perpetuated another favorite, and very crude, family story about a man who was "tongue-tied," which meant he had a speech impediment. He went into a shop selling candy and nuts and asked to buy macadamia nuts, cashews, and peanuts respectively. Each time when told the price, he said, "Oh no, those are much too high for me." Finally he left the store, but thanked the clerk for not making fun of his speech impediment. The clerk said, "Oh, I would never do that! I mean, look at my nose! It's so big, and everyone teases me about it, so I wouldn't make fun of someone else that way because I know what that's like."

The man replied, "Oh, is that your nose? I thought that was your peter, your nuts were so high."

Family humor was crude. But it is how I remember so many after-dinner conversations. Back then, it was what it was. I laughed with the rest of them.

Aunt Etoile took us all swimming at the nearby Painted Hills swimming pool. Out in the rural area where the pool was located, amongst the rolling hills that were "painted" green and purple on top and granite underneath, we swam and had picnics. Amidst the cheerful chatter at the picnic, Aunt Etoile came up with other jokes. She would always begin, "I heard the cutest story a few days ago..." We would immediately perk up our ears in pleasurable anticipation of the surprise to come.

"This is something that really happened in our hospital," Aunt Etoile began. "We had an older man as a patient who had diabetes. We took a urine sample every day to check his sugar level. But last week we had a new young nurse who started working at the hospital. Some of us, including the patient, decided to have a little fun with her." Aunt Etoile stopped to giggle; she had a wonderful 'hee-hee-hee' that was highly contagious. "So, *hee-hee-hee*, the patient was used to giving us a urine sample in the morning. He would get up, pee into the plastic cup, and leave the cup on his bedside table. A nurse would come in and pick it up. The new nurse got assigned to collected it one morning. Before she came in, we took away the real urine sample and substituted a cup of apple juice. The young nurse came in and picked up the cup. She knitted her eyebrows and said, 'This doesn't look right.'

"The old man said, 'Let me see that.' She handed it to him. He nodded at her. 'You're right. I'll run it through again.' And, *hee-hee-hee*, he picked up the cup and drank it!"

When Etoile and Grandma Miller visited us in London, Etoile showed her ability to make fun out of anything handy. Breakfast, instead of being a chore, became a magical delight as Etoile brought us a host gift of two egg coddlers. These small pots were made of white china with a pink floral pattern, and had metal lids with small circular handles on top where the tines of a fork would fit. Etoile showed us how to crack an egg into the egg coddler and add salt and pepper and a pat of butter. Then under her tutelage, I lowered the egg coddler, by way of the fork, into a saucepan of boiling water. The egg "coddled" in its seasonings while the water boiled, and after a few minutes, I inserted the fork through the handle again and gently lifted the pot out onto a plate for much-anticipated enjoyment of my "coddled egg." Etoile was known throughout the trip as Mrs. C.E.C., or "Chief Egg Coddler."

Just before Etoile's visit, Lisa had acquired a paperback book with instructions for various card games and tricks. It included a section on fortune telling. Every card foretold the future in its own way. Etoile spotted this book during a rainy Sunday afternoon. We had planned to go to a small amusement park, but the pouring gray skies precluded that. The usual card games of Rummy and Kings on the Corner held no allure; we had played them too often already. Noticing our restless disappointment, Etoile scanned the small book laying on the table. She retreated to her room and came back wearing a red and black checkered head scarf tied around her head like a gypsy. She had put on her largest pair of silver hoop earrings. She told us, "Now I'm going to tell your fortunes." She became solemn. "It will only cost you a penny." She added in a dramatically lowered voice, "But just because it is inexpensive…does not mean…it will not… come…true."

I still have the picture I took of Etoile that day with my Kodak Instamatic camera. She is wearing her scarf and dangling earrings. She and Lisa are sitting facing each other at our wooden dining table. There is a row of ten cards in front of them. Etoile's right index finger is pointing at the third card in the row. My sister sits with her chin propped on both hands, staring at the cards in fascination while Etoile revealed to her the secrets of her future. How easy it really is to entertain nine-year-old children. One only has to use what is at hand. It also helps to be as creative as Etoile, of course.

Years later, after Aunt Etoile had retired from nursing at the Normalville Hospital, she went back there for gallbladder surgery. She was well over 70 by then. She still knew most of the doctors and nurses there, and decided to surprise them. When she was asleep in the operating room, a nurse pulled up my aunt's gown and saw where Aunt Etoile had put a dotted line on her stomach, along with, "Fragile. Open with Care."

After Aunt Etoile woke up from surgery, she wanted to see her scar. She raised her gown and on her stomach was written, "Congratulations! It's a Boy."

33

COUSIN BRIAN

O n my father's side, my challenging cousin was Mark. On my mother's side, it was my cousin Brian. Brian was the middle son of Uncle Ronald, the restaurant owner. Like Mark, Brian was older than me so I looked up to him. He was at least as athletic as Mark, but while Mark was stocky, strong, and muscular, Brian was tall, thin, and wiry.

His sport was basketball, and he was a star player in high school. He religiously follows Indiana University's team to this day.

My Grandma Miller described Brian as "ornery."

We played Hide and Go Seek with him a few times. It was even less rewarding than playing with Cousin Mark. He was so quick and observant that when I tried to sneak back to home base, I inevitably heard, "One-Two-Three on Ann Lee!" Once again I had been caught.

He taught me to play Ping-Pong for the sole purpose of beating me. It was always a rout; nobody had faster reflexes than Brian. He was fiercely competitive. Although he was a tough Ping-Pong instructor, I did develop a killer serve with the tiny ball. I learned to whack it over the net, barely skimming it over with the speed of greased lightning. Later, with my peers, I won a few of our informal tournaments at parties.

He was even more competitive than Cousin Mark, if that was possible.

I honed my serve, I sharpened my quickness with forehand and backhand. I must have practiced, any time I got the chance, for about twenty years. Finally, at the age of thirty, the magical moment arrived. I was at a family gathering after he had gotten married. In the hosts' garage was a shiny new Ping-Pong table. I accosted Cousin Brian near the door that led out there.

"I want to play Ping-Pong with you again," I declared.

"No," Brian answered. And I never got that rematch.

Brian and his older brother, Tom, continued their family run restaurant and we made a point of going there on visits. When Hankley came on a family visit to introduce his fiancée, Brian turned to her and asked, "What's wrong with you?" He was as ornery as ever.

Tom, who was a kind man, tried introducing us to some of the other customers, mentioning that we were his cousins. Cousin Brian chimed in, "Very, very distant cousins."

During that same visit, we went out to eat together at Chucky's Restaurant out on the bypass. Cousin Brian and his wife had done me a few favors on the visit and I offered to buy a meal for them. Brian shook his head. "No. It isn't a big bill, so I'll get it. You can pay next time, when it's expensive."

After he paid our bill out of "the goodness of his heart," Brian turned to me and said, "Come back and see us again when you can't stay so long."

34

LISA AT HER WORST

O h, Lisa, Lisa! She of the pale, almost translucent skin, short wavy brown hair, green-gray eyes, and plump figure, was the bane of my existence. Maybe I was the bane of hers too. She competed with me almost from the day she was born. She never forgave me for being born first, and she never forgave my parents for birthing Hankley and taking away her status as the youngest. I am not sure whether she resented me or Hankley more.

When we were around eight and nine years old, we went through a phase of calling each other Mommy-kins, Daddy-kins, and Lisa-kins. We got this from the Archie comics where the character Veronica called her rich father "Daddy-kins." When I referred to my toddler brother as Hankley-kins, Lisa rolled her eyes. "No. He's Stinky-kins."

Lisa was the middle kid and, except when she could beat me out of it, always seemed to get the short end of the family stick. Dad was obsessed with the fact that she was overweight and he talked about it often, publicly and privately. He created a "weight chart," which he hung on the wall of our bedroom when we were five and six years old, so everyone could see if she was gaining or losing weight. There was much talk of Lisa's "figure" and every summer when we visited Dr. Middleton for our pediatric checkups, he put her on a diet. I wonder what it was like for her to see me eat candy and cookies and to be told she could not have any. Dad called me his "little princess." He called Lisa his "little dumpling."

My sister's meanness fully blossomed in Dusseldorf and advanced from there. Lisa saw that she could make me look bad by being extra charming and friendly, as I was very shy. My mother constantly criticized me for it, yelling at me to stop hanging my head and mumbling when she introduced me to her friends. She told me I made her look bad. Lisa saw a chance to add to the humiliation by being friendly to everyone. Not that she cared about the people she was friendly to. She simply wanted to be better than me. She succeeded.

She began to invite all the mothers of her friends to, "Come round for a cup of tea this afternoon." Lots of them did. Once she invited them, Mom was too embarrassed to un-invite them. So Mom ended up serving tea to Mrs. Edlund, Mrs. Rhodes, Mrs. Cox, and Mrs. Hostert. I still remember their names, and the way my American mother strained to make polite conversation with these women over English tea.

Besides making her look friendly and kind, this was a good deal for Lisa in another way. She got to drink hot tea with lots of sugar cubes in it. And the cookies and cake came out of the pantry. Lisa always had a monster sweet tooth, even worse than mine. Sugar was always a family drug of choice. As we all had tea, Lisa would announce, "I'm *beautifuller* than Ann."

One of the mothers smiled kindly and said, "I think you're both beautiful."

Lisa looked away and stuck out her tongue at me.

Lisa once declared, "Mom and I agree that you're the nervous type and I'm the calm, relaxed type." She started many conversations with Mom and her agreeing that I was deficient in some way. She once found out early on that I had been born with a faulty tear duct and jaundice. She had not had any issues at birth. She often reminded me that she had been a perfect baby and talked about my "birth defects." She also brought up my being left-handed for frequent discussion. As she got older and her vocabulary increased, she used to say, "You're *sinister*, because that's what 'left' means. I'm not, because I'm right handed. I'm *adroit*, and you're *gauche*."

Sometimes I responded in kind. When I learned the word "obese," I asked her what it was like to be that way. In those days, I thought all sisters and brothers were as mean to each other as we were. I was surprised when I found out this wasn't the case.

She coped with her lot by using humor, a strategy I learned from her. When my brother was old enough to talk on our phone, which in those days was a corded landline, he used to pace up and down the hall as he talked to his friends. Lisa watched him doing it one morning and observed, "Hankley has two generators in his feet that drive his mouth."

When I messed up, she was likewise delighted. As a young teenager I once came downstairs wearing pants that were far too short for me, showing not only my ankle socks, but bare leg above them. Lisa rolled her eyes. "Ann, are you expecting a flood?"

When I was learning to drive, she, of course, made fun of all my mistakes. One Saturday morning at breakfast when I was a newly licensed driver, Lisa noted, "When I drive with Ann, she's so slow that I can read every name and house number on every mailbox on Webster Road." She performed imitations of me driving up to a pothole, then into it, then out of it again, at a snail's pace, ducking down as I went into the pothole, inching forward, and finally coming up again.

"This is Ann driving on Webster Road," she announced, imitating the engine noise of our Ford Pinto. "Nrrr...nrrr...nrrr..." (She ducked down here, imitating me entering the pothole). "Nrrr......Nrrr......nrrr..." (Emerging from pothole, she sat up straight again). "Nrrrrrrrrr!"

Despite her mockery, I was a slow and cautious driver and remained so, possibly annoying people to this day. But I got a measure of satisfaction when it was Lisa's turn to learn to drive. She told me just before she took driver's ed that she was glad that I learned to drive first so she could "learn from my mistakes." But she made plenty of her own. When she took her driver's test for the first time she almost had a head-on collision with the driving examiner in the car. She had to take the test several times to pass. Her difficulty at getting a license pleased me.

She enjoyed her triumph over me when she was the first to have a boyfriend. She bragged constantly about how Andy Stein called her almost every day. Her conversations at age 13 always seemed to begin with, "And right there in class Andy turned to me and..." "...I almost died laughing when Andy said..." "...Andy is so funny! He told me what the weather was going to be. Andy says that tomorrow will be dark with patches of light by morning, with 100% chance of darkness again later in the day." She gave a trill of laughter with each of these statements.

One evening, she came home from Perry Middle School. "Andy and I hung out behind the school building. In the bushes," she smirked. "And he put his hand *there*," she smirked, indicating her crotch. "Then he went like *this*," she went on, and made a tickling motion with her fingers. Then she groaned. "I gotta masturbate," she breathed, lying down on her twin bed in the room at Grandma Locasio's that we shared. And she did. She lay down on her stomach fully clothed. She writhed and wriggled until at last she slowed down, stopped, and gave a long "Aaaaaaah."

I watched in stunned fascination. I may have actually begun to inhale through my mouth.

Other boys liked her in those days, too. She was still plump, but knew how to make the most of her looks. She styled her wavy hair into rippling curls. She applied makeup well. She had a small, slightly upturned nose and, more important, well-developed breasts. It was prestigious in those days to be "stacked." She told me with pride that several boys had checked her out by asking, "You've never had syph or clap, have you?" It was considered a great honor to be asked this. I did not have any boy interested enough in me to ask if I had had any STDs.

It was a full four years later before I got asked out. Finally, Steve, the fish fryer at the fast food joint where I worked asked me to go to the movie *Network* with him. He had winked at me several times as he stood over the frying oil. He had terrible acne, but at that point I wasn't in a position to be choosy. And he was reasonably smart and funny despite what the oil vapors were doing to his skin. When he finally asked me out I was ecstatic.

Lisa's response was, "So what? I got asked out by Andy in eighth grade. I beat you!"

Lisa could make up all types of insults on the spot.

The day I cut my bangs myself, as little girls are wont to do, I cut them too short. I had wet them before I took up the scissors; when they dried they stuck out, exposing my forehead. Lisa looked at my bangs, now perpendicular to my head. "They look like a roof. I'm going to call you 'House-Face.'"

One time when we were visiting my godparents, Aunt Gloria and Uncle Lewis in Chicago, Lisa informed Gloria, "You're my eighteenth favorite person."

Gloria, never one to get ruffled, responded, "Glad I'm in there!"

When she and I were leaving for school one day, I had a pile of books to carry from a long night of homework. Mom asked Lisa to help me by taking one or two of them. Lisa said, "I can't! I'm weighed down carrying this extremely heavy pencil!"

Mom laughed and didn't pursue it. I learned that day that life is not fair.

Lisa was not mean all the time. She often made the whole family laugh. She told us that worms aren't male and female the way people are. "Every worm has a male end and a female end," she explained. She was wrong; worms are hermaphrodites, with sex organs of both genders in their bodies, but not at their ends. But none of us knew that at the time. Mom asked, "How do you know which end is female and which end is male?"

Lisa knitted her brows and thought for a minute. "I don't know." Then she cocked her head and grinned. "But the worms know!"

35

MOM, OR CONSTANT CONTINUOUS CRITIC

om truly tried to be a good mother. She saw motherhood as her God-given duty. A heavy duty. When we were young, we were in church and Sunday school almost every week. She learned early to carry small pads of paper in her purse so we could draw pictures during the sermon. I didn't understand exactly what church was about. Mom said it was God's house, but I wondered why I never got to meet him there. One Sunday, the collection plate came around. Lisa had been learning her numbers in nursery school that week. She tossed a piece of paper with numbers into the plate, announcing to the usher, "These eights are for God." Mom yanked them out of the plate. "Don't embarrass me."

Mom was a devout Christian and a very religious woman like her mother before her. She made sure we had *The Children's Bible in Color* on our bookshelves. Being the avid reader I was, I enjoyed the story of the creation and the story of people blowing trumpets and having walls fall down around a city. And Daniel and his friends, being willing to be cast into a fiery hot furnace rather than give up what they believed in, was thrilling. It primed me to be inspired by Martin Luther King and Gandhi later.

In early childhood, I came up with imaginative questions for my mother, such as, "Are the clouds God's heads?" One time, I asked Mom if everyone believed in God like we did. She said no, because, for example, a person could be a Buddhist. I went away wondering why someone would worship boots. A preacher friend of mine chuckled over the "bootist" faith when he heard this story. "Remember, even bootists have soles."

I became aware of my mother's frequent wordplays during this time. I caught the wordplay virus without even knowing it. When my mother made beef stew for dinner she would say to me, "Do you want some stew, Pid?" When she made beef and noodles she would tell us it was "Boof and Needles." She taught me to sing the song, "What did Delaware, boys, what did Delaware? I ask you now, as a personal friend, what did Delaware?" The answer in the next verse was, "She wore her New Jersey, boys, she wore her New Jersey!" At bedtime we sang the 1940s hit Mairzy Doats. "Mairzy Doats and Doazy Doats and Little Lambs Zeedyvy…" The song explained midway, "If the words sound queer, and funny to your ear, just a little bit jumbled and jivey, Sing Mares Eat Oats, and Does Eat Oats, and Little Lambs Eat Ivy."

Mom might inquire, "There were two birds sitting on a fence, one named Pete and one named Re-Pete. Pete flew away and who was left?" We would answer, "Re-Pete." Mom responded, "There were two birds sitting on a fence…"

Mom would say, "I can cook eggs." When I replied, "So can I," she would ask, "Which one do you want me to soak?" Mom played with words all kinds of ways. She called coffee her "brown, life-giving fluid."

I found out that my cousin Cathy, who Mom babysat, has this penchant for wordplay as well. She may have picked it up from Mom or else she's just wired in the same way. On a recent visit to Cathy's house in Long Island, Cathy was preparing a meal. I told her that I was ready to help out. "I'm an extra pair of hands and feet," I reminded her.

"Okay," Cathy answered solemnly. "I want you to make the salad. With your feet." Cathy, years later, told me that she had read about people having chips implanted in them. She declared, "The only chips I want implanted in me are chocolate chips." She was related to my mother, for sure. Chocolaholics, both of them.

Although she was playful with words, Mom could be stunningly and bitingly accurate about my sometimes careless speech. I once told her after losing and then finding my wallet, "When I was looking for my lost purse, it was in the last place I looked!"

My mother raised her eyebrows. "I hope so."

Not that Mom was always rational. I once, as a teenager, left a mess in the kitchen after making tacos. I went to my bedroom, turned on some rock and roll on the radio, and completely forgot about the kitchen chaos. Mom discovered the dishes splattered with ground beef and salsa, and came and tapped on my bedroom door to ask me if I was going to come clean up. The way it came out was, "Ann, are you still in the kitchen?" Dad was passing by and knitted his brows. "If you think she's in the kitchen, Betty, why are you looking for her in the bedroom?"

Even Mom and Dad's suburban bridge-playing buddies got a little crazy sometimes. They were master tournament bridge players, and enjoyed playing Duplicate. In Duplicate Bridge, partners went from table to table, playing the same hands of cards as their predecessors. Therefore, one could not blame a poor score on bad cards. When my parents were playing Duplicate, couples would socialize happily between hands…until it came time to play. Then, an almost funereal silence would descend. There was so much at stake. One night, a foursome was finishing a conversation after the other tables in the room had gone dead silent. The last thing a loud woman called out was, "And did you ever try doing it in the bathtub?" Shocked silence. It turned out the woman was talking about cutting her kids' hair.

When my parents played bridge, I sometimes overheard stories they told that they hadn't told me. They had met another couple years ago, I found out. Both husband and wife had been married before, and they had four children between them that they brought into the new marriage. Sometimes the couple ate at a family restaurant with all four kids. When a friend came into the restaurant who hadn't met the children, he asked, "What are their names?" The wife responded, "Rosemary, Richard, Richard, and Rosalind."

A most peculiar look crossed the man's face.

The couple could almost hear him think, "How unimaginative!"

36

WHAT IS HUMOR, ANYWAY?

learned about humor from my family. I was strongly motivated to understand it. Storytelling in general, and humor in specific, were tremendously important to everyone. To belong, to be accepted and appreciated, storytelling skills were essential. I watched and listened to my father. His tone, his timing, his terminology were all absorbed by me mostly not by direct instruction, but by observation and imitation. It was a more complicated education than I realized at the time. It had its difficult moments. When I got it wrong, I got puzzled looks or laughs not at my wit, but at my foolishness. But I kept on trying. The subject was too important to give up.

Once, I gave my mother a birthday card when I was about eight years old. It said, "Do birthdays bother us? Heck, no! We're only 21…or so!" This humor, such as it was, would only work if the card came from one adult to another. It made no sense coming from a child. I saw her puzzled face and wondered why she didn't laugh; after all, the card was cartoonish in appearance.

My father, fortunately, was quick to understand what had happened. Then he did something kind. "You think it's bad to get a joke wrong? You should have seen how dumb I looked as a kid! I didn't just miss out on jokes. I had them played on me! Once, when I was thirteen years old and working as a dishwasher at Kelly's Lunch Counter in downtown Upperville, a couple of guys who were waiters came to me and said, "We're almost out of meat. Go to Hellman's Café and ask if you can borrow their steak-stretcher." So I ran off across the town square to the café. I found Tommy Hellman and asked if he'd loan me his steak-stretcher..

"Tommy told me, 'Oh, I had it, but I let Howard borrow it at Wyler's Cafeteria, so you'll have to go there...'"

Dad said he ran all over town that day chasing the fictitious steak-stretcher. They did that to all the new guys at restaurants in town. It was an initiation of naïve boys into the sometimes brutal world of young men. Boy Scouts take their new kids on snipe hunts for the same reason.

People tend to do what's done to them. Dad later told me of a memory he wasn't so proud of. There was a boy in their sixth-grade class who was cross-eyed. His name was Jerry. Jerry had other things wrong with him too; Dad wasn't specific about what those were, except that Jerry was "slow" and didn't have great social skills. One night, the boys in Dad's gang invited Jerry to go with them on a camping trip. Jerry, wanting to belong, eagerly accepted. When he went to sleep, Dad and his friends dipped Jerry's hand into a bucket of warm water, causing him to pee in his pants. Dad looked ashamed thirty years later as he told me that story. I thought about it every time us kids got pocket money in Upperville and decided to "go down Jerry's" who had a five-and-dime store a few blocks away. I remember him as a quiet and kindly man. He never married. He seemed to like us kids. I didn't mind him being cross-eyed.

Tempering humor with kindness is a trial and error process. I've heard people say glowingly of some little kids, "She (or he) doesn't have a mean bone in that little body!" That was not true of either my father or me. We were both born with a mean streak or else we learned it early. Whatever kindness my father and I showed was learned. It was an acquired habit, which came about only after choosing to act unkind ended up in experiencing bitter consequences.

When Dad told me about Jerry, I saw deep remorse and sadness in his face, even decades later. *Don't do it,"* he seemed to wordlessly beg of me. *"Don't treat other kids like I treated Jerry."* His entreaty didn't work when I was young, but finally I got the message. Years later, I requested and sometimes received forgiveness for my "Jerry moments." Thankfully, I have learned how to offer amends to others. I have also learned to grant compassion and grace to my clueless young self, and thus was able to move on.

I finally figured out the rules of humor. First, while children can laugh at the same thing over and over again, with adults it's only funny the first time. Also, children tend to take things literally. Here is a good example: At the age of three, I was with our nanny, Brenda. She was in a rare good mood, humming a Beatles tune softly and getting ready to clean house. She wanted me to stay in the enormous bedroom/nursery and keep myself occupied. She didn't want me under her feet while she cleaned. I happened to be riding Dobbin, my rocking horse, at the time. Brenda said to me, "You stay here with Dobbin. Keep an eye on him." So after she left I got off the horse and pressed hard on one of Dobby's eyeballs. "There," I said out loud. "I kept an eye on him."

Later, in junior high, our class made fun of this juxtaposition between metaphorical and literal. Our theater teacher told us to act out figures of speech. So we said, "He rolled his eyes," and mimed removing an eyeball and rolling it like a bowling ball. I told a classmate, "Pull yourself together." She acted as if she were grabbing pieces of herself out of the air and attaching them to her body.

After I learned the art of humor, one of the joys of watching little Hankley grow up was observing him go through the same process. One evening, having dinner at my Uncle Ronald's cafeteria in Normalville, Hankley was listening to the usual after-dinner jokes that his father and his two teenaged sisters were telling. Hankley decided he wanted to be part of the fun. He broke in, "I know a joke! Why did the car stop?"

We all stared blankly and shrugged our shoulders. "Tell us."

Hankley beamed. "Because the TRAIN WAS COMING!" Then he looked around at us with a puzzled face because nobody laughed.

After a few seconds we realized what Hankley had attempted to do and we doubled up with giggles. We tried to explain that for a joke to be funny, the ending had to be a surprise. He didn't quite get the concept of joke telling…it's an acquired skill. Years later, I heard a description of humor as a "benign violation." Both parts matter. It has to be benign, or harmless, to be funny. It also has to involve a violation of what's expected. Hankley's car stopping because a train was coming was benign, but not a violation.

It took both Hankley and me a long time to wrap our minds around the *double entendre* found in so many sex jokes. It is still mysterious to me why *double entendres* always seem to be about sex. "Engineers do it efficiently," or, "Comedians do it standing up," or, "When cooks do it, it's hot." And so on, with everyone knowing what "do it" means. There was even a Swedish sex whodunit, I heard. Apparently the butler was the only one who didn't do it. I couldn't resist that, but it does prove my point.

Then there was the birthday card my parents got my Great-Aunt Phoebe that took me until I was an adult to appreciate its serial *double entendres*. "For your birthday I wanted to get you a THINGAMAJIG for your WHATCHAMACALLIT. But I didn't know what size your DOOHINKY was!" Rule of comedy: You'll usually get a laugh if you go for the dick joke.

The most famous family joke most often told became part of our folklore. It wasn't just the content of the joke, but the fact that it was told at a potluck supper with Great-Aunt Phoebe there, and she laughed so hard she wet her pants and had to be taken home to change. The joke got repeated, along with Phoebe's response, many times over the years.

It involved a traveling salesman who got constipated and went to a doctor who gave him a potent laxative pill that would work with a vengeance in 30 minutes. The salesman, a gregarious guy, got caught up talking to a client on the street and lost track of time. With minutes to spare he panicked, ran to his hotel, and pushed the up button for the elevator. Horrors! It was out of order. So he rushed up the five flights of stairs to his room. By the time he reached the third floor, the pill had taken effect. He kept running, and at last, reached his destination. A few moments later he heard a knock on the door. His heart sank; surely it was the manager coming to throw him out. But he was wrong. It was the janitor's son holding a mop. The young man had a pronounced lisp. He told the salesman, "Don't worry. The manager wanth to thay, it'th perfectly all right. Thith kind of thing happenth sometimes. That'th from the manager.

"Now, thith ith from ME. If you have to go to the potty, don't run up five floorth to your room, you thun-of-a-bitch. *Thtand thtill!*"

That was my training in humor. These jokes would, I suspect, not be well received these days and many of them would be considered disrespectful. I am merely passing on what I saw and heard that made the adults around me laugh and consequently impressed me. At that age there was no judgment involved, only an admiration for what the older folks did.

Those who speak wistfully of "youth culture," and reminisce about childhood days long past, sometimes forget how earnestly young people long to be adults. It was that longing that caused me to remember the jokes and stories that mattered so much to my family. I figured if I could remember and tell stories like they did, then maybe I would be accepted as one of them. So I practiced my storytelling skills, with greater or lesser success, until I mastered the art of entertaining my family well enough for them to take me seriously as a humorist. Ironic…but true.

One source of my early instruction in adult humor came in a frequent nighttime family amusement. It began in 1966 when I was seven years old. After we finished dinner, Dad would ask us to read Charley Weaver's *Letters from Mama*. Weaver was a 1950s comedian perhaps best known for his appearances on the game show *Hollywood Squares*.

Weaver's real name was Cliff Arquette. He appeared on the late-night Jack Paar show before it became the Johnny Carson show; before it became Jay Leno's show; before it became Jimmy Fallon's show. Arquette would dress up as the old man "Charley Weaver" with a fedora and small round eyeglasses. He would whip out a piece of paper in front of Jack Paar and announce, "I had a letter from Mamma today." Off-camera, he said in an interview that he did this because he found it hard to memorize lines and got very nervous trying. If he could read a "letter from Mamma" life was easier for him because he just read the letter off the paper.

As children, we would not get the jokes at all. This was adult humor. It wasn't raunchy. It was just humor that only adults would understand. It required living life as a grown-up. But Dad loved to hear us read the jokes in our little-girl, solemn British accents:

> "Dear Steinway, (*Mamma always wanted me to be upright and grand*). It's election season in Mount Idy, and everyone is running for some kind of office. Leonard Box ran for mayor. When he quit running, he was in Mexico. Mount Idy's county fair is this week. Wallace Swine has the concession stand. His sign says, 'Dine with Swine.'"

Or there was this one:

> "You know, son, ever since Grandma Ogg got struck by lightning, she can get television on her glasses. Last week we all went over to the Oggs' house to watch the Yankees baseball game on her glasses. But Grandma had allergies so bad, the game was rained out."

It made sense to an adult in a ridiculous way. I remember the shortest letter the best.

> "Dear son, I was going to tell you all the news and also send you the fifty dollars I owe you, but I see I have already sealed the letter. Love, Mamma."

We got a lot of mileage out of that phrase "sealed the letter." In later years, I would write letters to my brother saying, "I wanted to send you tons of money, but I see I have already sealed the letter. I had some terrific porn to forward to you, but I see I have already sealed the letter!"

REALITY RUDELY INTRUDES—SECOND GRADE

O f course our home leaves always ended and that meant going back to Europe, my father going back to work, and Lisa and I going back to school. This was particularly hard because my father changed work assignments and locations so often. After spending two years in Dortmund, we moved to the town of Dusseldorf. That meant going to a new elementary school, or primary school, as the British called it.

The Dusseldorf Primary School was where I entered second grade. Years later, I calculated that I attended each school an average of one and a half years. My new teacher, Miss Crisp, believed that imagination was something to be stifled. We were to follow all directions exactly. Mathematics was taught by a rule book. I was unhappy and spent whole days not talking to anyone. Miss Crisp, like many of my teachers thereafter, believed in public humiliation as a punishment for lessons badly done. My work was often held up as an example of what not to do. My lack of physical coordination also became an issue. At the end of every day, we held relay races for exercise. Each day, the fastest and most coordinated children were praised, and the slowest and clumsiest, like me, were castigated. My classmates rolled their eyes in despair when I was assigned to their sports teams.

I was allowed to take candy, when I had it, to the Dusseldorf Primary School to share. On the days I had candy, I always had friends and didn't have to play alone. I told Mary how much better liked I was on the days I had candy. Mary told me that my real friends were those who were there "every day, not just when you've got sweets." I learned in those days that dope pushers are never lonely as long as they have a stash.

The school was divided up into four "houses" for competition, much like children's summer camps get split up into "tribes." Good schoolwork earned a child a "house point," which was taken to the headmaster's office. I did have one or two days when I proudly conveyed my tiny blue plastic disc to Mr. Hughes' office for a brief commendation. Our houses were Blue, Red, Yellow, and Green, and they were named after famous British seamen. This was because Mr. Hughes was a veteran of Her Majesty's Navy.

My house was Scott, the Blue House. There was also Cook, the Yellow House; Hudson, the Green House; and Drake, the Red House. My best friend Isabel was in the Green House. The worst bully in class, Mark Northcott, was in the Red House and constantly bragged that his house was better than any other. Classmates exchanged heated words among themselves about which house was the best. At the end of the year, Scott House won the trophy and a royal blue ribbon was tied around the huge base of the silver cup in our honor. Mark Northcott narrowed his eyes and pursed his thick lips in disappointment.

In addition to faculty-sponsored rituals and contests, Dusseldorf Primary School children made up their own routines. It was the custom on Mondays for boys to pull up girls' skirts and say, "Washing Day!"

Older kids would come up to me and ask me to "say hello." When I said hello, they answered, "Fatso!"

On October 1, when I had been at the school less than a month, my classmate Margaret came up to me and hit me on the arm, saying, "Pinch punch, first day of the month!"

On November 1, I paid her back by doing the same. She responded with, "A punch and a kick, for being so quick!"

I never could keep up with those kids.

I withdrew as much as possible. At night, I imagined monsters under my bed. Out of the corner of my eye I could see every shadow in every closet, moving. I checked under the bed every night for ghouls, goblins, and ghosts. Sometimes, I woke up in the middle of the night and checked again. The monsters under the bed were almost as bad as the real people I had to try to get along with during the day. What I heard my mother declare was that I was "full of fears" and "very immature for a seven-year-old."

I had less energy than most children when it came to meeting the demands of school and the hazards of the playground. Moreover, my natural introversion was a huge problem for the family. Early social isolation is noticed these days and some children, at least, are taught social skills. Not me. My mother blamed me, as always, for my social deficiencies.

On one visit back in the United States she finally took me to a child psychologist. I thought that seeing that doctor was my mother's punishment for all she hated about me. The doctor asked me why I was causing so much pain to my family and why I would not try harder to do what other children did so easily. Time spent with him was time taken away from the days of fun with my grandparents. He asked me what subjects in school I did not like and I said, "Arithmetic." He then asked me to do some arithmetic for him between sessions. I was right. The doctor was a punishment.

That year, I discovered a new source of pleasure. I had so little of it otherwise. Stuffing a pillow between my legs, lying on my stomach, and wriggling against the pillow brought me a strange sensation in my body like eating sweet-hot mustard did on my tongue. I called what I did "wiggle-worming." Then one night, my mother walked in and saw me. If my physical development caused fury, my physical activities caused horror. She did not become angry or hit me. Instead, she told me to pray to God to show me how this was not a right thing to do. Good Christian girls never did that. We were not supposed to feel that kind of pleasure. It was wrong. This encounter didn't stop me from wiggle-worming, though. After we left Dusseldorf, my life force reasserted itself. I could not stop, and did not have the willpower to refrain. I just lived with the guilt. I also got clever about not getting caught.

I note here that my mother never had any grandchildren. Perhaps there is poetic justice in that.

We had a swing set in our backyard in Dusseldorf. I tried to do some kind of balancing trick. I succeeded once, but I recall that after doing it, I felt out of control and out of balance, so I did not try it again. My mother asked me why. I told her I did not want to because I was afraid of getting hurt. She became very angry. "For heaven's sake, Ann Lee!" she stormed. (Like many mothers, when she got angry she called me by both my first and middle names). "You've done that before! Why in the world won't you do it again?" There is a part of me that still does not comprehend her anger.

I prayed to God later that day to end my life and take me to heaven. I stood condemned by my mother. I had failed childhood. I did not measure up. I was physically defective. I was socially no good. I asked God to quietly let me die that night and not wake up the next morning. I had lived seven years and that was enough. I explained to God that the world would be a better place if I were not in it. I spent the rest of the afternoon in my room alone, thinking about death and praying for a peaceful and quick end.

What I know now was that there was a reason for my being a slow developer. I was born with jaundice and the doctors treated it using a method that was later discontinued because it caused problems in motor development. I was slow to learn to walk as a baby. I did not learn to swim or ride a bicycle until I was nine years old. My mother often reminded me of my deficiencies in this regard. As I mentioned earlier, I can still hear her shouting as I walked down steps at age four, putting both feet on each step. "One foot on each step! Not two! Do it right!"

I prayed similar prayers for many years. I was often puzzled that those prayers were not answered because after all, Mom taught me that God always answers prayer. In later years, after increased physical development made suicide attempts more possible, my mother took me to task for committing such a grievous wrong. "You let God decide the time of your demise! Not you!"

I wasn't in a great place to argue with her at that point, but I remember thinking, "*I did let God decide that a long time ago. In those days you were God to me.*"

38

CHALLENGES CONTINUE, MARY HELPED

Humor helped with life's challenges. I was lucky to have it. Other than the occasional bright spots, my time in Dusseldorf was difficult. The principal at the Dusseldorf Primary School, Mr. Hughes, had a scorching temper. Mr. Hughes had been the equivalent of a drill sergeant in the British Navy. I am sure he cured any smart-mouthed recruits he may have had. He was thin and imposingly tall in his suit and tie, with buzz-cut gray hair and a salt-and-pepper handlebar mustache. His black beady eyes were usually narrowed in slits as he investigated each daily incident of misbehavior, great or small. One afternoon, he strode into the hall to begin our afternoon assembly. Apparently a few hand towels had been tossed on a restroom floor.

He held up the dirty towels and just breathed audibly and slowly for a few minutes. His face slowly flushed. I knew what was soon to erupt. I felt my heart slamming again and again, against my chest. "YOU WILL NOT THROW TOWELS ON THE FLOOR!" he roared thunderously. "I WON'T HAVE IT! DO YOU UNDERSTAND? I... WILL... NOT... HAVE... IT!"

The last thing I remember was wondering if he was going to stomp off the platform and come after us with his fists. A few minutes into his remarks, I disassociated.

When my father heard me tell of what Mr. Hughes did, he said, "I probably don't yell at you kids enough. If I yelled more, you'd get tough.

You'd get used to it." My father never followed through on this idea. Perhaps there is a God after all.

Mr. Hughes was also responsible for the White Line. This was a line painted on the playground about a hundred yards from the school door. If anyone crossed the White Line, they would be in "deep trouble." He also gave orders that when lining up for afternoon assembly we must be in order of tallest to shortest. Miss Crisp would call us to get into formation by shouting, "Girls! Line up in heights!" We were not allowed to sit next to chosen friends in assembly or at lunch, but assembled, again, in order of height. There was no talking allowed on the way to or from assembly. Talking in the hallways, as was the case at my earlier school, was a serious offense.

Another school ritual occurred in the fall. We were expected to collect leaves at the end of recess. We were assigned to pick up twenty leaves and deposit them in the trash cans before we were allowed to come in out of the cold. A teacher could count our leaves to be sure we made quota.

Dusseldorf was also the place I sought to join the Brownie Scouts. There was only one Brownie Pack and many girls, like me, wanted to be members. I was intrigued by the snappy brown uniform with its straight yellow tie with a gold elf on the tie pin. Some of the older Brownies had earned the Golden Bar merit badge, sewn over the shirt pockets, and triangular special interest badges on the sleeves. I had gotten hold of a Brownie Handbook to prepare myself. The book told me I could anticipate a "very big welcome" in my new Brownie Pack. I was excited. The girls in school whose uniforms sported the most badges held high status. I envisioned the day that I would have both badges and admiration. One afternoon I went to a Brownie meeting after school with a friend who'd invited me.

One of the older girls came up to me and said, "Hey! Who said you could join?"

To this day, I get nervous at any club meeting where I'm not a member. Although in almost every case since back then, the group members have been more than gracious.

I remember Mom coming to pick me up. Apparently a teacher had called her. I assumed she'd said to my mother that my being there was a mistake and I wasn't allowed to witness the secret ceremonies of the Brownie pack. "You can't be here," she said. "You shouldn't have come to the meeting. The Brownie leader just told me you have to leave. We're going home."

I was led away as the Brownies assembled around their large, brightly colored plastic toadstools for the secret ring dances. Elves, Fairies, Gnomes, and Pixies all had their special group, their special place in the room, and a special song. It was all so deliciously new and unknown. I remembered reading a story in my Brownie handbook where some friendly girls sang at their Pack meeting, *"We're the Fairies, Bright and Gay, Helping Others Every Day!"* But the door closed behind me, and I was not allowed to see the Brownies dance. My mother led me away by the hand. The brown double doors closed behind us. Part of me still wants to go back through those doors and watch the girls circling those giant toadstools. In my imagination the dancing is accompanied by merry laughter.

My mother would not discuss this incident with me afterwards. She seemed to find it annoying. "Stop whining about it," she finally snapped at me. After that, I never brought it up again.

The next school day, a Brownie named Sharon Lane who was two years older than me and had a ton of merit badges, approached me on the playground. She stuck her tongue out. "We're never going to let *you* in, you know."

So much for the "very big welcome." What I came to realize is that what is in print and envisioned in theory and could be earnestly desired by whoever wrote the handbook, may not match the reality of a situation.

Our tenure in Dusseldorf lasted only a year. There was only one saving grace about that year. Her name was Mary. Mary was the third nanny we had and the best one. She was 28 when she came to us in Dusseldorf. She was recently divorced and felt the need to get away from her home in

England for a while. Mary had short strawberry-blond hair, blue eyes, and rosy red cheeks. She smiled a lot and laughed often. I always felt that she genuinely liked us, and we returned the favor.

My father interviewed her and they liked each other instantly. Mary was not just loved by children, she attracted everyone she met. I recall how Lisa and I played tricks on her. We would put hairbrushes in her bed so when she crawled between the sheets at night, the bristles would tickle her feet. She would do the same to us. She told us stories, and then listened carefully when we told her our own tales. It did not matter whether they were invented, or whether we were relating the events of a school day. I could tell Mary things I could never tell my mother. Mary was a wonderful listener. To this day that is the greatest gift she gave me. She listened.

Mary played games that to us were simply entertaining, but which required us to use our brains. We played "I Spy" where one of us would "spy" something in the room and say, "I Spy with My Little Eye, Something Beginning with B." Then the others had to guess what it was. This game developed my power of observation, which was not one of my strong points at the time.

We played another game called, "I Packed My Bag," which began, "I packed my bag, and in it I put... a toothbrush." After that, the next person would say, "I packed my bag, and in it I put a toothbrush, and some soap." As the game went on, each participant would have to repeat all the prior objects in the bag before coming up with her own object for the "bag." And so it went on. I owe part of my good memory to Mary's activities.

Mary came from the English county of Lincolnshire and had a distinctive British accent unique to that region. She also had relatives in the county of Norfolk. She could mimic the accents of all her relatives and we found this hilarious. She told us her uncle in Norfolk would greet her by saying, "*Hah-loh! 'Ow ye gettin' on?*" In Lincolnshire, Mary said they had a unique way of saying, "Have you got a light on your bike for when you go out tonight?" A Lincolnshire yokel might say, '*Have ye got a loyt on yer boyke when ye go out tonoyt?*" Lisa and I were good mimics. We would practice the Norfolk and Lincolnshire phrases Mary taught us, and repeat them at the family dinner table, causing much hilarity.

When the school year ended in the summer of 1967, we bid a tearful farewell to Mary. I recall her waving goodbye to us and seeing her cry. I would like to say I cried too, but that would be a lie. Some events are beyond tears. What came out of my mouth was, "Well, I suppose we'll never see *her* again!" My mother and father thought this was a very hard-hearted remark. But I had already moved enough times to have doubts about the permanency of any relationships. I had developed a hard, stoic attitude as a protection against separations. And I was learning not to invest myself in people. It was better to just go through the motions and not even try to make any close friends. I withdrew socially and read a ton of books. Learning to take the risk of knowing someone and being known did not come until later. I found that friendships came hard and went away easily.

My great good fortune is that we did indeed see Mary again. In later years, she visited us in our various homes and after a while she married again. She and her husband David would then visit us as a couple. Mary just turned 78 years old and we have been in contact for 48 years.

Just about the time I had made a best friend in Dusseldorf, a girl named Isabel Hostert, it was time to move on. I hated leaving Isabel because it had taken a long time to find a best friend at the Dusseldorf Primary School. Isabel's mother was a Louisiana Catholic, and her father was German. Isabel was raised Catholic. She thrilled me with stories of her First Holy Communion where she wore a white dress and a veil. She ate a flat wafer that was supposed to be the real body of Jesus, and she drank a sip of real wine. The way she described it, she was queen for the day.

After the First Holy Communion service, her family threw a big party in her honor. The American church that our family attended had no such rituals. I found our church in Dusseldorf, as well as the Methodist church in Normalville, Indiana, mind-numbingly boring. Even my friend Angel's Sunday school teacher in Upperville gave out free candy...we didn't even have that. Isabel's Catholic Church let her wear a white princess dress and participate in mysterious and exciting ceremonies. Although this was after Vatican Two, her church still had a Latin mass. To the smell of incense swinging and smoking in the censer, they chanted, "*Gloria Patrie Filho et Spiritu Sanctu...*" with their chants echoing off the stone walls.

Everyone else's churches were more exciting than mine.

A SURPRISING TRANSITION WITH LOTS OF COMMERCIALS

W e came back to Dusseldorf only briefly after our home leave in America. We thought we would be there another two years. Then the reality of Mary's absence hit me hard. Lisa and I did not sleep well at night. The thought of returning to the dreaded Dusseldorf Primary School without Mary to come home to at the end of the day was weighing on us. But before school began, we got a surprise. My mother was pregnant again. Nobody expected that. She did not like her German gynecologist, whom she said was very rough with her and made her bleed. She described him as "an old Nazi." She wanted to return to the United States permanently. She wanted to have her baby there so there would be no doubt about the child's American citizenship. And she was tired of speaking German every day.

To our utter delight, instead of returning to school in Dusseldorf, we climbed aboard an airplane again and came back to Indiana. My mother warned us that this would not be another vacation. We would have to go to school in America now.

Mom enrolled us at Pittman Elementary School in Upperville. We would live in Upperville with Grandpa and Grandma Locasio and attend school down the street from their house during the week. We would spend weekends with Grandpa and Grandma Miller in Normalville. After attending British schools, I found Pittman School to be extremely easy except for the math lessons. But even the math was easier than math at the British army base schools I had attended thus far. At the age of ten, Lisa and I once thumbed through a workbook for fifth graders in an American drugstore. One of the topics covered was "What Are Fractions." We exploded in giggles. We had been doing fractions for three years. So schoolwork was, for once, a breeze. And I got to come home every afternoon to my grandparents' house. We played with the girl next door, the non-angelic Angel, after school. We had no homework, so the end of the school day meant unlimited playtime until dinner.

We watched a lot of television. American television seemed vastly better than British television. We watched cartoons every morning before school and every afternoon when we got home. Our grandparents had a color television, a novelty in those days, and the brightly colored cartoons were sheer heaven. I still remember some of their names: Popeye the Sailor Man, Top Cat, Mighty Mouse, Hercules, Space Angel, Superman, Clutch Cargo, and Roger Ramjet. I also remember the endless commercials inserted between the cartoons. Madison Avenue had learned well how to market to children by the mid-1960s. I recall begging my grandmother to buy sugar-laden cereals like Quisp, Lucky Charms, and Apple Jacks. I learned to sing every advertising jingle urging their purchase. My grandmother used to tease me because at night, when both adults and children were watching TV, when the commercials came on I told everyone, "Ssh!" I loved them as much as the shows.

I asked Grandma Locasio to help me save fifteen Apple Jacks box tops so I could send off for a free red, apple-shaped Bowl n'Mug Set with Apple Jacks for eyes and a smiling mouth. It was a long project. We moved to England before we had enough box tops. So once we were gone, Grandma Locasio bought Apple Jacks for her mother, my Great-Grandma McClain, to eat…she saved all the tops. It was a joyous day in London when my Bowl n'Mug Set arrived. It was also a joyous day for Grandma McClain, who had gotten sick of eating Apple Jacks.

I can still recall singing along with Bugs Bunny, "Make friends with Kool-Aid, Make Kool-Aid with friends…" Although I loved the ad at the time, it was frustrating too. It featured a little boy named Tommy who was all alone in his house until, guided by Bugs Bunny, he made a pitcher of Kool-Aid. Suddenly, lots of children appeared out of nowhere to drink Kool-Aid with Tommy. The ad ended with Bugs Bunny saying, "Tommy's made so many friends, there's no Kool-Aid left for me. So I'll make some Kool-Aid!" We learned early on to seek solutions to problems in products. I seem to recall laws being passed that restrained some of this marketing. I remember wondering why, when I made Kool-Aid, friends did not appear like they did for Tommy.

Before cigarette advertising on television was banned, every American who saw this ad could complete the phrase "Winston tastes good" by saying, "Like a cigarette should." There was a cigarette ad jingle that sang, "You can take them out of the country, but…you can't take the country out of Salem!" I watched every ad with careful attention and tried to persuade my mother to switch her brand of cigarette to Tareyton, Kool, Lark, Viceroy, or Lucky Strike. But she had developed brand loyalty to Kent, "the world's finest cigarette." Don't let anyone dare say that advertising doesn't work.

Even while I was happy to be living with my grandparents while my father looked for a job in the USA, I was again finding it hard to make friends. I recall two boys named Bobby and Billy. Billy would bump into me at recess and say, "Hey kid. You're a pig. Say you're a pig or I'll hit you." I remember Natalie, a tall, slender and blond member of my class, pretty and vivacious, who was a total contrast to me. She was always surrounded by friends. I wondered how she did it. Natalie never had trouble with bullies. They didn't come near her. She later went on to make cheerleader and class secretary. I wrote to her years later as an adult, when we made contact through a mutual friend. I told her how much I had admired her in my youth. She wrote back, "You sound like a very nice person." She should have added, "Even though I don't know who the hell you are."

I experienced elation through sugar, though, once again. Hostess Twinkies were my friends. I wonder how I ever survived after eating that many Twinkies. When I was in my twenties I heard a story (it may be apocryphal) of a college student who adored Hostess Twinkies. When he graduated, the day he left his dorm room he crawled under his bunk bed and nailed a Hostess Twinkie to the baseboard. He came back a year later, was admitted to the room by the students living there, and asked permission to look under the dormitory bed. He found the intact Twinkie still nailed there. The power of preservatives. Maybe Twinkies helped me look young for my age.

That short six months in Upperville allowed me to experience just once in my life what every privileged American kid gets to have every year: Halloween and Valentine's Day. Halloween was unforgettable. I wish I had saved my Batman costume. I would have had it bronzed by now. It was the one and only perfect costume. For a kid that felt anything but heroic, that night I was mighty and invincible. I trick or treated with my father, so the bullies couldn't get me. More important, the idea of knocking on all the neighbors' doors and being given free candy by everyone who answered was a sugar addict's dream. Later, chomping down on my bag full of candy corn, Milk Duds, Snickers mini bars, and other free sucrose-laden loot, my heart rejoiced. I wondered why it couldn't happen more than once a year. Once a week would be better. (In the same way, the first time I attended a Fourth of July celebration I thought that if I ruled the world I would make sure fireworks went off every Friday).

Valentine's Day was almost as memorable. Somehow I thought I would be the only one giving out cards, which would make me very special. It was somewhat anticlimactic to realize everyone did it. Still, I enjoyed getting all those tiny cards sprayed with glitter from everyone in my class, even those bullies: Bobby and Billy. I thought it meant that everyone liked me. I treasured the illusion for the single day it lasted. The fruit punch and sugar heart cookies were also fine by me.

I spent seven months in third grade at Pittman Elementary School. Behind the scenes, my father was looking for a job in a steel company in Indiana or in a nearby state such as Illinois, Ohio, or Pennsylvania.

However, Booz Allen & Hamilton (the same company Edward Snowden later worked for) urged him not to resign. My father explained to some executives at that company that his wife was tired of speaking German and was urging him to get a job in the United States. Someone at Booz Allen & Hamilton made him a novel offer. They proposed that he go to work for them at the British Steel Corporation (BSC) in their London office.

The BSC needed the Standard Cost System there just as the steel companies in Germany had needed it. My father had become an expert on Standard Cost. He could once again make presentations, waving his hands around, using thrilling terms like "standardizing costs" and "variances" and "coefficients" in ways that made my eyes glaze over and ask whether we could please stop talking so I could go out and play.

My father had become a superstar efficiency expert and Standard Cost was his gig. It was a concept only an accountant could love. I now understand that it was a method a business could adopt to know what its costs were at every point in time so it could minimize them, control them, and make a profit. My father was fond of saying, "There is no way to make money if you do not know what your costs are." That part at least makes sense. The rest of Standard Cost is still a fine cure for insomnia as far as I am concerned.

The company liked my father and his work; they also knew he liked living in Europe. So the company urged my father. "Go to London and implement Standard Cost for us at the BSC. They speak English in London and your wife will no longer have to speak German." Their begging and cajoling paid off. Once again, my mother's desire for a permanent home in the United States vanished like a dream at dawn.

40

INTRODUCING HANKLEY

My brother started out small.

I thought little Hankley would never arrive. "Late October or November," my mother had promised in 1967 while we were living in Upperville. But he apparently liked my mother's cozy womb, because he continued to park himself there and dig in. Finally, the doctor induced labor. I wonder if Hankley was aggravated by that.

"He just doesn't want to be born!" my mother marveled.

In later years, we would point out to Hankley that there was a reason he was such a procrastinator.

My father once said it was too bad that Mom could not have taken "Lego Pills" so that Hankley, taking his sweet time about emerging into the world, could build houses and gas stations *in utero*. Never mind. Once Hankley got born and was old enough not to swallow the pieces, his Lego love affair began. He built endless contraptions with gears turning in both directions. In the summertime after we moved back to the United States, he built giant mazes with stair-steps that went from one section to another. One spring, he put an unfortunate toad he'd captured from the front yard into his maze. The toad had to hop through the maze, prodded on his backside by a grinning Hankley. At maze's end, the toad would see a clear view ahead and would hop forward to the longed-for freedom. Then dismay struck! Hankley had built a wall of clear plastic Lego for the poor toad to bonk itself into. Eventually Hankley, a kind person underneath his devilishness, let his toads go after much "a-mazin'" amusement.

I once told my mother that compared to most boys, Hankley was pretty cool.

Mom exclaimed, "But he could be a little dickens!"

After she said that, I recalled the time that Hankley, curious to see what it would look like, spilled ink all over the dog. What he got was a dog with blue spots on him. Charlie didn't mind as far as I could tell, and Hankley was delighted. A blue-spotted dog was such a novelty.

Then there was that day in London when three-year-old Hankley went into the kitchen, closed the door, climbed up on a stool to the kitchen sink, turned on the faucet, picked up a saucepan, filled it with water, and poured it on the floor. Repeat. Repeat again.

That action was repeated until I opened the sliding door and found an ecstatic Hankley, standing on a stool in two inches of water.

At eight years old, I could not foresee any of this. At first I only saw a picture of sleeping innocence and miniature fingers and toes that looked like those of one of my larger dolls. This was accompanied by the sound of soft breathing. I could see that despite his slightly flushed face, he was a beautiful baby. I am not a romantic about babies. Most babies, to my mind, are not all that cute and some of them are rather unpleasant looking. But Hankley, notwithstanding my bias in the matter, was a lovely child. The beautiful baby became an impossibly gorgeous toddler and later a handsome man. He eventually ended up as a top notch engineer at a high-powered tech company. I am convinced that Hankley was born for a charmed life. Hankley was the baby prince, the promise fulfilled, the bright and shining star.

In his early days, however, he was not a lucky person and it was difficult for me to be around him. He had constant colic. I can still remember the exact sound of his crying. My mother had postpartum depression with him as she had after birthing her other two children, so Grandma Miller came to live in Upperville for a while and help take care of Hankley.

"After I had you, I was depressed for six weeks," Mom once told me. Only years later did she tell me that had been true for all of us. Even so, as I went out each morning into the sometimes harsh world of school and heard my baby brother crying, I sometimes wished I could be like tiny Hankley, at home wrapped in a warm blanket in my Grandma Miller's arms. At other times, I wished that we had purchased Hankley from a store so we could fish out the receipt and send him back.

My parents looked at their new child, and in him could see the child's future and anticipate the great work that their offspring would one day perform to change the world. That child's eight year old sister didn't have this perspective. All I saw was a chaotic, perpetual need for taking care of a helpless creature who could do nothing for himself. Most of all, he was a terrible playmate. He couldn't even talk to me. After all the buildup of excitement over "the new baby," he was a big letdown. I failed to understand why my parents would bring a being into the house who made that much discordant noise. I never knew what Hankley would do next or which orifice he would choose to do it from. And the odors he could produce were astounding.

Lisa and I once overheard my father saying that she and I were our parents' two miracles, and Hankley was more like a surprise. My mother had to work very hard to get pregnant. For a long time, she couldn't ovulate. There was a "blocked plumbing" issue of some sort, like being reproductively constipated. Finally, the proverbial pipe got opened up. I got out, and my sister escaped behind me fourteen months later. It seemed that the hole closed, until in 1967 there was some kind of a leak and Hankley sneaked through, too. This caused my father to rush to the doctor's office for a vasectomy. We often teased Hankley about being the "Family Shock." It didn't faze him. He was born believing life would work out for him, and it always seemed to.

When he started school, he was tracked immediately into every Gifted and Talented program available for staggeringly advanced children. He got picked for fourth-grade Robotics, Future Engineers and Scientists,

World Leaders of Tomorrow, and "Emperors in the Making." (That last one is an exaggeration, but not by much). And he was obscenely lucky. When he was just nine years old, he entered a contest, the one and only sweepstakes he ever entered. The sweepstakes were sponsored by a brand called PDQ, a type of chocolate powder that dissolved in milk or could be used as a topping. It was mostly sugar with a faint overtone of cocoa. The only reason Hankley entered was that it had to do with chocolate. The young chocoholic had to say which way he liked PDQ best, and declared on his entry, "PDQ is best on ice cream."

For his effort, he won third prize, $165. It came in a large glass jar, and it was all in dimes. We all had to go down to the local town Pick N Pay grocery store so that Hankley could receive his prize. The store manager, Mr. Lally, had to set up a special PDQ display for the occasion. He was not thrilled by this extra work. A town newspaper reporter showed up to interview Hankley and take pictures of him inserting dimes into the Pick N Pay bubble gum machines. The headline the next day blared: **Bubble Gum Bandit Empties Machines; Rides off into the Sunset!** There was a picture of Hankley turning the handle on one of the machines. The other picture showed Hankley, Mom, and Mr. Lally in front of the PDQ display. Mr. Lally had a very forced smile on his face. Hankley never entered another sweepstakes.

We went home that night and played cards. Hankley beat me.

We teased Hankley, of course, but he learned to give as much as he got. One morning, before I was fully awake and was waiting to eat my breakfast, Hankley played one of his favorite games with me. This annoying game was called, "What Would You Do?" He would pronounce my name with a lilt in his voice, which indicated that he was about to break into giggles. "Ann," he smirked, "If someone gave you ten dollars, would you be pissed off?"

I looked at him like he was nuts. "Only if they owed me twenty."

Hankley persisted, "If someone made you smoke ten cigars at once, would you be pissed off?"...or... "If someone dropped ten thousand bombs on you, would you be pissed off?" His examples became more and more absurd, which made me more and more exasperated, much to Hankley's delight.

He also enjoyed playing a game called "Would You Rather..." He would chortle, "Ann, would you rather drink a truckload of boiling medicine or have someone tie you to a rocket and shoot you to the moon? You can't say neither one! You have to pick one!" Years later, I discovered, on a trip to Toys R Us, that someone had marketed Hankley's idea. There was a game on the shelves called "Would You Rather?" Apparently Hankley wasn't the only one tormenting his family with it. He loved to concoct hypothetical situations. It was his engineer's way of discovering how the world works. One time, when he was only ten-years-old, he was at the swimming pool with Mom. She gave him money and told him he could buy refreshments at the concession stand during rest period. "Can I ask for anything I want?" Hankley asked Mom.

"Sure, Hankley," Mom said. "Don't be shy. Just walk up there and ask for what you want."

"Can I say anything? Anything at all?" Hankley persisted.

"Yes, I told you, that's okay," Mom encouraged him.

Hankley cocked his head. "Is it okay if I ask him 'How big is your dick?'"

Mom should have said, "No, because then I'd be pissed off."

41

LIFE IN LONDON

After six months of living in Upperville, Dad accepted the new European assignment with Booz Allen & Hamilton. While somewhat mollified by the idea of living in an English-speaking country, my mother was once again about to be separated from her extended family in Normalville. She would be far away from the beer-drinking, coffee-sipping, Six-Tricks card games. She would miss seeing her family, which included: Aunt Gladys and Uncle Don, Aunt Phoebe and Uncle Gilbert, Aunt Lillian and Uncle Henry, Aunt Barbara (who was more like her sister than her aunt as they were close in age), all her cousins, and her mother and father.

My mother was not happy that after eagerly anticipating reintegrating herself into that network of kinfolks, she once again had to board an airplane again and head back to Europe. Once again she had reason to resent my father's actions. Once again there were marital storms about which I knew nothing. What my mother had once thought was going to be a three-year stint in Wales had turned out to be an indefinite residence across the Atlantic Ocean.

Hankley was only five months old when my father made his decision to stay with Booz Allen & Hamilton and take the family to London. My mother now had to manage to travel with three children instead of two and similar to her journey to Wales several years earlier, had a child in a crib on the wall of the airplane. The cabin pressure in the airplane hurt Hankley's tender ears and he bawled most of the way. I wonder if my mother felt a helpless sense of *déjà vu*.

I did not find out until later how many times my mother threatened to leave my father, get a divorce, and bring her three children back to the United States. Fortunately, my parents sheltered me from the quarrels and the worries they would have caused me, only telling me about them when I was an adult. Even with all the pressures and challenges, my parents presented us with a united front, at least when it came to where we would live.

As we left our grandparents at the departure terminal in Indianapolis, I saw my Grandma Miller dab her eyes with a lace-edged handkerchief. We took a short flight to New York, and boarded the British European Airways (BEA) jet at Kennedy Airport.

We moved into an apartment building called The Lodge. In British terminology, it was called "a block of flats." Our apartment was huge. Located in the Royal Borough of Kensington, which also housed Kensington Palace; it had four bedrooms and two and a half baths. We sometimes heard the Queen's horse guard galloping down our street early in the morning. The buildings around us were elegant, mostly apartment buildings like ours, built in the Victorian era and style. They were several stories high with large windows and were painted pale yellow, pastel orange, light grey, or off-white. The building across the street, however, was sugar-candy pink. I wished the candy part had been real.

To our great joy, moving to London meant we were closer to Mary, our former nanny from our days in Dusseldorf. "I guess we'll never see *her* again!" I had once proclaimed, and how joyously was I proved wrong. She had gone back to live in her hometown of Spalding, in the county of Lincolnshire. She now owned and ran a shop where she sold women's clothing and various yarns, wools, cottons, knitting needles, crochet hooks, and other feminine merchandise. She came to London fairly often to buy items for her shop, and when she did, she would always stop by our London apartment to see us. I remember one time in particular when Mary visited us. We had been in London a few years by then, and Lisa had just gotten a puppy.

By that time, Lisa had become both a voracious reader and a dog lover. Actually "dog lover" is too mild a term to describe it. She was almost feverishly in love with dogs. Whenever she came upon dogs when we went for a walk in a nearby park, she would stop and make a fuss over them. She could do a passable imitation of a dog's bark. She tried to get the dogs to bark back. When Lisa was not relating to dogs, she was reading about dogs. She also read anything else she could get her hands on. She read children's books and dog books, William Shakespeare's plays and dog books, a medical encyclopedia and dog books. She once took a break from dog books to read a book written by a retired prostitute, from whom she learned some interesting lessons about human reproduction and the antics surrounding it. I do not know to this day where she got that book.

Lisa was so dog-crazy that when we got a miniature black French poodle called Beaujolais (Beaujo for short), Lisa decided she wanted to eat her supper on the floor out of a bowl, just like Beaujo did. Mom humored her, and solemnly set a dish of stew on the floor for Lisa next to the dog's dish. Before Lisa could lean down on all fours and taste the stew, Beaujo ran up and devoured it. Thus ended that phase. For a while afterwards, though, Lisa still did not finish a sentence without barking like a dog. "I had a good day in school today. I got all my math problems right. *Arf-arf-arf!*"

Unfortunately, Beaujo turned out to be a neurotic biter, so we had to get rid of him.

42

LISA MEETS THE DOG SHOW CHEAT

B y the time Mary came to see us and to meet Lisa's new spaniel puppy, Charles, Lisa was about ten years old. In addition to loving dogs, she was still a voracious reader. Her latest volume was the *Popular Medical Encyclopedia* where she devoured columns of small print written by doctors about various conditions affecting human beings. Mary, a dog lover herself, instantly fell in love with Lisa's furry, brown, floppy-eared puppy. Due to living in London and going to British schools, Lisa and I had both acquired British accents. When Mary told Lisa how lovely the puppy Charles was, young Lisa combined her voracious reading, her love of dogs, and her newly acquired medical terminology. She eagerly responded to Mary's compliment in her girlish British accent, "Oh yes, Mary, he is a *lovely* little dog, isn't he, but we think he's a *homosexual!*"

Charles came from Mrs. Judy Bentley, a breeder of Cavaliers. Mrs. Bentley was Hungarian, but she had married into British gentry. Her husband had a great deal of money. The man had promptly died and left her his fortune, along with unlimited time to breed her beloved spaniels, attend dog shows with them, and pass endless amounts of time with other women of leisure. One such lady was the Countess Czernin (pronounced Cher-Neen). Her son was, according to Lisa, a "flaming queen." He pranced around the dog show ring in tight black pants and rhinestone-studded sunglasses. He smoked his cigarette in a holder, and would call out to the

Countess in a well-bred, but nasal voice, "Oh, Mummy, look at the dear little *puppeeees.*" Lisa got to go to the dog show with her.

Mrs. Bentley groomed her dog, Twiggy, on a folding table; when the dog show ended, she wiped down the surface and replaced the Cavalier with liquor bottles. She rounded up the Countess and her other friend Peggy Talbot, a rather severe looking woman with gray hair she wore in a bun and a large, imposing, and slightly obese figure. She walked with a cane. "Peggy," called Mrs. Bentley in her Hungarian accent, rolling her r's, "Would you like a drrrrrink?"

Peggy frowned. "Oh Judy!" she boomed. "I really shouldn't! No, I shouldn't do it at all! BUT I WILL!" And she came walking over to the liquor table as fast as she could. If she hadn't had the cane to slow her down, she would have been running.

Mrs. Bentley was a cheat. Twiggy was a black-and-tan Cavalier. Cavaliers are not supposed to have any white spots, but Twiggy had several. Not wanting to lose points with the judges, Mrs. Bentley applied mascara to all of Twiggy's white markings. Due to the multiple white spots, this took a little time. Twiggy would sometimes get bored and try to lie down and take a nap during the long cosmetic procedure. Mrs. Bentley would cajole her, "Oh Twiggy *darling, don't* go into a *coma.*"

After cheating with her dog and drinking heavily, Mrs. Bentley and Lisa would pile the folded-up show table, the picnic basket, dogs, and themselves into Mrs. Bentley's tiny Triumph Spitfire convertible for the long trip home. On one occasion, an intoxicated Mrs. Bentley took her hands off the steering wheel to light one of her tiny cigarillos, and promptly bashed into the rear end of the car in front of her. The angry man got out of his car and walked over to Mrs. Bentley. "Now look here, lady!" he began.

Mrs. Bentley held up her hand, rolling her r's as always. "My name is not lady. My name is Mrs. Bentley. And how could you drrrrive so badly? You should go back to Drrrrriving School! Have you even *been* to Drrrrriving School?"

The man was so bowled over by her verbal assault that he retreated, got into his car, and drove away in his badly damaged car. Mrs. Bentley got away without a scratch.

Mrs. Bentley got away with just about every ruse. Al Capone, Vince Ponzi, or top management at Enron could have learned a thing or two from her.

THE NEW NANNY AND HER PRACTICAL JOKES

Soon after we arrived in London, a new nanny named Carol came to care for us. Carol was small and squat. She had short, straight blond hair and vacuous blue eyes and had the accent of her home county of Yorkshire. She pronounced "cocoa cups" as "kaw-kaw koops." She wasn't the brightest light bulb in the pack, although she was sweet; and she loved my baby brother. She would coo and cluck while giving Hankley his bottle and say in her Yorkshire lilt, "He's a looov-ley beh-bee." She was good with infants, but didn't quite know what to do with us. We asked her hard questions such as, "Why should I have to eat my main course before my dessert, as long as I eat both?"

She would default to, "Because we just do it that way."

We retorted, "But why?"

I still think it's a good question. Especially now as an older lady who insists that life is short so she always eats dessert first.

Carol kept us amused by telling us about jokes she and her friends used to play on each other. She said that while she was a single woman working in a Yorkshire office, she shared an apartment with three other girls. They all played pranks on each other. Someone once ran bath water and one of her roommates sneaked in and turned off the cold water faucet, leaving only scalding hot water. Not being the brightest button in the bag, Carol saw no problem in planting this idea in children's minds. Luckily,

163

we never tried it. We did take delight in Carol telling us about putting salt in someone's coffee. After we tried that on Dad, he commanded Carol to immediately stop giving us ideas. It did not occur to Carol that relating every practical joke she ever played, to eight-and nine-year old children, was a bad idea.

For a while Lisa and I both went crazy playing these practical jokes. We ordered and received Onion Flavored Chewing Gum from a special offer out of a children's comic book. We gave some to Christopher, the neighbor boy who lived in the basement of our high rise apartment. At the time, we thought it was hilarious to see Christopher take off running to spit the gum out.

We had a Joy Buzzer that we ordered from a different comic book. It was a round plastic gizmo with a button that simulated an electric shock when we held it and shook someone's hand. We also had a Whoopee Cushion, an inflatable rubber cushion that, when hidden under a regular cushion and sat on, deflated with a massively loud farting noise. We thought that it was awesome. But anything to do with farting was awesome. But then came the day that Lisa gave me what she said was cinnamon on toast, but was actually chili powder. That was a lesson in empathy. I was not so quick to play mean jokes thereafter.

Carol stopped teaching us practical jokes, but she taught us other skills, which my mother frowned upon. Carol had a friend named Anne. She was a nanny at the home of Lord and Lady Phipps who lived up the street. Lord Phipps may have been an English Lord, but there was nothing lordly about his house or his children, both of which existed in a state of chaos, piles of toys strewn everywhere. His children had an insolent manner with strangers too.

Anne was no help. She constantly looked for excuses to beg off work and nip down the street to hang out with Carol. She called our home at least once every day. I used to enjoy hearing the phone ring and rushing to answer it in excited anticipation of who might be calling. I was often disappointed by the dull voice of Anne, who pronounced her own name "Ahn," asking in her drawn-out dopey drawl, "Can I speak to Carrrrrl, please?" The two of them once baby sat us together when my parents went on their usual Saturday night dinner date. They had the idea of borrowing our binoculars to spy on the young "fellas" at the Academy House college student apartments across the street.

My mother despised Anne. She told me that Anne had low morals, so of course I found ways to be around her to satisfy my child's curiosity about what someone with low morals was like. I wondered what it was about Anne that so repelled my mother; eventually I just got bored with her. After Anne left the Phipps's employ, Mom told me, "I saw Anne working at Derry and Tom's department store today. She looked about fifty. That's what happens when you live such a wild life." She pursed her lips in distaste. Mom, ever the dutiful Christian, was always ready to impart a moral lesson upon her children.

But I found Carol and Anne's conversations fascinating when they talked about the "fellas" they were dating or with whom they were hoping to date. Carol's boyfriend Dave, who barely said hello when I finally met him, was apparently, "good with his hands," when on a date. At least, that's what I gleaned from eavesdropping on Carol and Anne's conversations.

I liked the blond, affable George better when he came to the house one night to pick up Carol for an evening out. When I came in the room he stood up and shook hands. Carol approved. "He's a very polite fella," she simpered. Unfortunately, George was a smart man, so the relationship did not last long. I doubt that "Carrrl" could carry on enough of a conversation to keep him interested. But she and "Ahn" could go on for hours about their "fellas."

It went like this: "He said…" "And then she said this back! She did!" "*Ooh!* She *didn't!*" And on and on it went.

I owe "Carrrl" and "Ahn" thanks. They taught me how to gossip.

44

THE SIXTIES...AND LONDON'S WORST CAFETERIA

t was 1968. Given the King and Kennedy assassinations, Vietnam war protests, the feminist movement, and Civil Rights unrest occurring in London as well as elsewhere, it is amazing how sheltered I was from all these political realities. I recall my father talking about the feminist Germaine Greer with utter scorn when she refused to wear a wedding ring when her husband would not. He sneered at the women who burned their bras and never mentioned the reasons behind such acts. When my mother mildly protested at the way, in beauty pageants, women were "paraded around like cattle" my father snapped, "Good heavens, Betty, be quiet. You sound like the Women's Lib!" When we asked about protest marches, my father dismissed their agenda, saying, "Oh, they just like to protest for no reason. Everybody shows up, and then they all decide what they're going to protest about that day."

Dad was a product of his generation. He defended his country and won his manhood, and when he returned, his home was his castle and he didn't like having his comfortable sense of order questioned. When I took Women's Studies courses in college and passed on what I was learning, he sneered at me. "No society in the world has women in charge. Do you know of any? I don't."

His attitude pushed me to study further. I went on to discover the matriarchal structure of some ancient societies. I am sorry to say, however, that for a long time I was too intimidated to face his scorn. Only later, did I realize the fear that lies behind anyone's rigidity, which allows no dissent, including my father's. We had a few shouting matches over politics before he died.

But he could not entirely shelter us from the realities of the times. I recall vividly the bright sunny Sunday that Carol took us along the Notting Hill Gate road to Kensington Palace Gardens. On the way back, we encountered an antiwar street demonstration. I didn't understand the chants then, but recall being intrigued by the call-and-response pattern of the crowd protesting Vietnam. "What do we want?" "Peace!" "When do we want it? Now!" We walked alongside them for a while.

Suddenly, Carol gasped, "They're setting fire to the road! Keep Hankley safe!" In a panic, she shoved me against Hankley's baby carriage. My entire leg was scraped and it hurt. She never asked if I was all right. It wasn't the last time I felt shoved aside in the family, but that time was the most memorable. Luckily the protest didn't become dangerous. We race-walked out of there as fast as we could, dodging the crowd on the sidewalk.

Carol sometimes took us swimming at the neighborhood indoor pool on Saturdays. She would bathe with Hankley in the kiddie pool at Kensington Public Baths while Lisa and I swam. After exhausting ourselves for a couple of hours with swimming, splashing, turning handstands and cartwheels in the water, racing each other, and diving, we would be ravenous. Because Carol's salary wasn't large and Mom wasn't willing to pay for expensive meals, we often ate at the cafeteria called The Buttery at Barker's department store. Barker's had eight floors and two restaurants. The chic one called the Penthouse was on the top floor. It had gleaming silverware, white tablecloths, and played soft music. That was where Mom had lunch when she shopped in Kensington High Street by herself or with Dad.

The Buttery had tile floors and occupied the windowless basement. When Carol and we three children shopped, the Buttery was all we could afford. The walls were battleship grey and stained with both the passage of time and food that had been spilled or thrown there. The lime-green booth seats were cracked and faded. They usually had morsels of scrambled eggs and crumbs on them as the staff rarely cleaned anything. The Penthouse had wait staff. The Buttery was a cafeteria because its clientele could just do it themselves, thank you very much. When we went through the line, I would politely ask for a cup of tea to accompany my sandwich. The middle-aged woman pouring our tea wore a perpetually bored expression as if the Buttery would be a great place to work if it weren't for the annoyance of having customers.

When I requested tea she'd sigh, "Right, ducks," pronounced DOOKS, or "Here you are, luv," pronounced LOOV. She would impatiently splash some tea into a cup from a huge, dull-colored metal cylinder. She then forcefully slid the cup to me so that a third of the contents spilled into the saucer, necessitating my lifting up said saucer and pouring the tea back into the cup once I got to the table.

Nevertheless, we were so hungry from swimming and so unaccustomed to good service in those days that we cheerfully accepted the plastic-wrapped cheddar cheese and tomato sandwiches jammed between sorry slices of white bread and accompanied by the lukewarm tea provided by Barkers Buttery.

Lisa and I bathed together until we hit puberty. Mom saved on the water bill that way. We didn't mind. We had bath toys galore, including a bucket, spade, and small plastic bowls. The plastic bowls became our "coffee cups" when we played the Barkers Buttery Game.

I usually pretended to be a demanding American tourist, of which there were many in London every summer for us to observe. "I wanna cup of coffee! And make it snappy!" I would playfully snarl my commands in a loud American accent at Lisa, who played the part of the cafeteria staff.

"Right, *Dooks*," she would sigh in perfect imitation of the bored lady who had served us that day. She dipped a cup into the bucket, which was our pretend "coffee pot." She used enough force that water slopped over the side of the tub. "Do you want whipped cream, *LOOV*?" she would demand. When I answered "yes," she took the bright red plastic spade and dug it into the piles of bubbles in our bath, scooping up a shovelful, then inverted it and slammed it down on the bowl, making a spitting noise. "PPPPP!" Bubbles and water went flying into the air.

It was an excellent game. It ended only when my irate mother entered the bathroom and saw the results all over the floor.

45

INTRODUCING ULLA

After Carol left my parents' employ, we had a German nanny named Ulla. Ulla is one of the most common names in Germany, derived from the name Ursula. Ulla was 23 years old and a petite 4 feet 11 inches, with long, straight, shiny black hair, brown eyes, a turned up nose, and flowing sex hormones. In later years, my mother described how Ulla would come to her late at night in tears, worried about possibly being pregnant. She would confirm to my mother that she remembered what my mother had told her last time. Yes...she had meant to refrain, but when her current boyfriend, Berndt Muller, kissed her, she just melted. She assured my mother that she was going to obtain birth control very soon, but it wasn't really necessary because she would never let it happen again. And she didn't, until the next time the handsome Berndt Muller got a bit randy.

Eventually, her other boyfriends Karl, Heiner, Josef, and Johann faded away, and she married Berndt who was a hyper-masculine, broad-shouldered guy. He fathered Ulla's three children. All of Ulla's kids had glossy magazine-cover good looks like their handsome father and petite mother. They may have grown up to be movie stars.

I did not know until years later about Ulla's passion for men, but I always knew she was passionate about life. So it made sense that she would be passionate about her boyfriends. Ulla had definite likes and dislikes and did everything to extremes. She always had a cigarette tucked between her index and middle fingers; she was even a passionate smoker. She showed us how to blow different sizes of smoke rings. She could also whistle through her front teeth. I admired this talent to no end.

I once sang a song to Ulla that I learned at school. I sang the song with gusto to a tune we were learning from a Gilbert and Sullivan operetta. "The flowers that bloom in the spring, tra-la, the flowers that bloom in the spring…" Ulla wrinkled her nose and cut me off. "Ann, you sing like an old car in the morning."

Lisa loved that. It inspired her to find new ways to insult me. Every time after Ulla compared me to an old car, whenever I started to sing, Lisa would say I sounded like a cow. "Moooooo," she would bray, tilting her face up in a bovine imitation and drowning me out.

I persisted, though, and sang in my middle school junior choir, high school choir, and as a young adult in our church choir. I'm okay as long as I can blend in with about a hundred others.

I've retired from singing now. These days, I only sing in the shower.

Ulla had a standing joke with my brother when he became old enough to talk. "Hankley, will you take me dancing tonight at the Hilton Hotel?"

Hankley would say in his toddler voice, "Yah. Take you dancing, Ul-la."

At night, after she had bathed him and dressed him in his pajamas, Ulla would ask, "Are you ready to take me dancing?"

Hankley would say, "No. Too tired, Ul-la. Let's go 'morrow."

Hankley was an early walker, but a late talker…and even later with his toilet training. In that, as in most things growing up, he was a procrastinator. Even when his speech had become relatively articulate, he would come to Ulla and say, "Ulla, I did a wee-wee in my diaper. I need you to change it."

Ulla, fed up, would scold, "Hankley, if you're old enough to talk about it, you're old enough to use the toilet!"

Ulla loved to walk and she and little Hankley walked from Notting Hill Gate to Marble Arch and back, a distance of several miles. At age three, it was a bit much for Hankley's short legs. He complained to Ulla on the way home, "Ulla, he needs a bus." (Hankley said "he" for "I" in those days).

Ulla urged him on. "It isn't far, Hankley! Keep going!"

About a mile later, Hankley stated firmly, "Ulla, he needs a taxi."

Ulla took English classes and her English was actually very good. She did go to the greengrocer once and asked for "sleeveless oranges." When everyone laughed she said, "Oh, I'm so sorry. I meant 'ceaseless oranges.'"

One gift Ulla gave me was learning to wait patiently by doing it creatively. The first (and only) Christmas she was with us, she bought 24 small inexpensive toys and Christmas decorations. She wrapped these small articles in alternating red and green tissue paper and tied them together in one long string, and then hung the whole thing on the wall in the hallway. Lisa and I took turns opening one package each day. Whoever didn't get to open a package that day got to open the door on the colorful cardboard Advent Calendar that hung next to the packages.

Even after Hankley was born, Lisa continued trying to push herself ahead of me, over compensating for the fact that she was not the first born...not the oldest child. One way she did this was by insisting that she'd be first to open a package when December started. She got her way. But that left me with the last package on Christmas Eve, an awesome silver spray-painted angel with a gold halo that also held a magic wand. So it was perhaps a New Age angel.

Ulla taught us the joy of anticipation with the Advent candle, which had red notches all the way up from top to bottom, marked with the numbers 1 to 24. We also burned this seasonal candle a section at a time until it was all burned down by Christmas…the excitement grew and grew as the candle got shorter and shorter. We did get distracted by dinner table conversation one night and burned two days by mistake, so we had supper by electric lighting instead of candlelight on December 12th.

Ulla probably got her Christmas angels, candles, and small gifts for a bargain price at the nearby Portobello Road flea market. Ulla adored Portobello Road. She was an inveterate bargain-shopper. Portobello Road and Ulla were the perfect symbiotic relationship. The vendors loved her, and she loved their stuff. She also met one of her boyfriends at the market in the days before she fell in love with Berndt Muller, which further endeared her to the place.

When she had only been with us a week, she picked up an old fox fur there for under a dollar. Ulla loved to haggle and bring prices down. In this case it likely wasn't hard. That fur was mangy. The fox it came from might have been a despised, ostracized sly-fox relative nobody liked. Mom said it was probably infested with fleas, but Ulla loved it and wore it constantly all winter. Every time my mother saw it she shuddered.

Ulla was artistic too. When I got invited to a school friend's hippie party, Ulla helped me dress in the perfect hippie costume. We were almost the same size. I wore her teal bell-bottomed slacks, tie dyed aqua shirt, and eight beaded necklaces. Ulla also borrowed my mother's wig and I wore that. It was an authentic looking costume. The only thing wrong with it was that I had to wear Ulla's bell-bottomed slacks. Her waist was tiny. The elastic around my middle was skin-tight. Still, it was worth it. I looked like a true hippie and won the "Best Hippie" prize.

I came home with the box of chocolates wrapped in a blue ribbon and exulted to my sister, "Look! I won first prize!"

The corners of Lisa's mouth turned down sourly.

"That's only because you wore a wig," she snapped.

I often wondered in those days about Lisa's inability to congratulate me or wish me well for anything. And heaven help me if I got sick. The day I came home early from school with the flu and a hundred degree fever,

Lisa had to carry my books home at the end of the day. She walked into the London apartment where we lived and demanded, "What do you think I am, a hall porter?"

Occasionally, although not often enough, I got to see Lisa mess up. When we went to get our DPT vaccinations, the doctor told us that DPT stood for diphtheria, pertussis (whooping cough), and tetanus. Lisa later told a surprised family friend she had gotten vaccinated against "whooping cough, tetanus, and diarrhea!"

BADGES, BLAZERS, AND BLACK TIES

Over time, I came to appreciate London's cultural treasures like the Tower of London, Madame Tussaud's wax museum, Big Ben, Hampton Court Palace, and the British Museum. But at the age of eight, it was mostly about school and home. When we arrived in London, my mother enrolled my sister and me in a private elementary school. We wore a school uniform. We had light blue checkered dresses and navy blazers with the dark blue school badge on the right pocket. Socks were knee-length and white, closed-toed sandals brown. We wore straw hats called "boaters" in the summer, with the blue striped school ribbon around them.

In the winter semester, we had long sleeved blue shirts, gray pleated skirts, and a blue and black striped school tie. The girls as well as the boys wore ties. We learned how to tie them. Sometimes we had to tie them quickly if gym class ran late, so I practiced a lot to be ready for that. I can still tie a man's tie. Perhaps I should put that on my resume. I could become a rich guy's valet, except that most rich guys don't wear ties anymore.

Norland Place looked nothing like an American school. It was surrounded by row houses on Holland Park Avenue, where it still stands. It always had a stellar reputation. It still does. "A place at this school is like gold dust," said one guide to British schools. Norland Place had high standards from the beginning, when it was founded in the 1800s by its first headmistress, Emily Lord. I never saw a picture of Emily Lord, but I envisioned her as tall, wiry, rail-thin, strict, dark-eyed, thin-lipped, frowning, and walking with a cane, which doubled as a stick to use on lazy students. Perhaps I formed my picture of Miss Lord from the way I felt as I descended down the front steps at the side entrance into the school's coat room.

There was a front door, but it would have been unthinkable for pupils to use it. It was out of bounds to all but parents and distinguished visitors. The school had few windows. The halls were narrow and dark. There was no drinking fountain. To get water, a student used a beat-up lime green plastic cup that hung by a chain next to the sink. Everyone used the same cup. With the hefty fees my parents paid, I wonder why nobody suggested that the headmistress could have provided more than one cup.

At the "parents meeting," the equivalent of the PTA, there was a sherry party. The girls in Class Five, (fifth grade) the top grade at the school, had the honor of serving the trays of sherry to the parents. Dad was one of the parents pouring out the liquor. "Imagine that," Dad marveled later. "In America, you'd never have fifth graders serving sherry, or a bartender at the PTA." Dad thought it was wonderful. Serving alcohol in as many places as possible would always be wonderful to Dad.

The fourth grade curriculum was taught by the formidable Mrs. Perrum. When I first arrived at the school I was placed in a class two grades lower than the top class that Mrs. Perrum taught. I had only one fervent desire which was: *Never, never end up in her class.* Every teacher had something called "cloakroom duty," where they supervised us while we waited in the normally rowdy coat room for the school bus. It was the one time I had extended exposure to the dreaded Mrs. Perrum. When it was her turn for coat duty, there was utter silence in the room. She never told us not to talk, but nobody did. Lisa once responded cheerfully when Mrs. Perrum told her to tie her shoes, "I like to tie my shoes."

Mrs. Perrum answered grimly, wagging her bony finger, "You'll do as you're told whether you like it or not."

Some girls in her class once got rowdy and broke some pencils. Mrs. Perrum made them sit around the trash can for two of their lunch periods and sharpen an entire large box of pencils in complete silence while she sat and watched them.

I did well in the class where I was placed and, with incessant drilling at home from my mother, learned the multiplication table up to 12 x 12. When the following year came, I was in Miss Gilbert's class, one class below Mrs. Perrum's, happily acing all the quizzes on multiplication. School had never been so easy. I was sure it was because I was brilliant. Not only that, but word went around that Mrs. Perrum was going to retire at the end of the year. Safety!

Three weeks into the school year, my mother came to find me one afternoon while I was doing homework. "Mrs. Garnsey called. She says Class Three is too easy for you. She wants you to move to Class Four. A double promotion. Congratulations!"

Class Four was Mrs. Perrum's class.

47

ACCELERATED ACADEMIC ACHIEVEMENT...OR ELSE!

The specter of a year with Mrs. Perrum looming caused me to feel as if a great rock suddenly landed in my gut. My life was over. The horror had begun. I was sure that my new class would be full of punishments that would make hellfire and brimstone look like a trip to the Dairy Queen. I told my mother I didn't want to do it.

She said brightly, "But you'll get to leave school sooner!" Why I bought that line, I don't know to this day. Maybe it was the honor of the thing. But the day my mother and I climbed the creaky wooden stairs to the top floor of Mrs. Perrum's lair, I mean classroom, I realized there was no escape. My fate was sealed. My goose was cooked. My happiness had gone twenty-two-skidoo. And so on.

My last day in the kindly Mrs. Gilbert's class went by all too quickly. After school, my mother and I were now face to face with Mrs. Perrum. She was as tall as a skyscraper. And then she said, "I'm looking forward to having you in my class. I'm *really* looking forward to it."

Maybe she didn't eat small children for supper after all, I considered. Still, years later, when I read a book called *The Teacher from the Black Lagoon*, I thought of Mrs. Perrum. And I did in fact have some intense moments in her class. When I made mistakes on an easy English grammar exercise, she told me in front of the whole class, "It's not like you to use such bad grammar." I dissolved into tears.

I remember being told the night before a quiz, "*Woe betide anyone who doesn't know their French verbs by tomorrow.*" I didn't know what kind of "woe" Mrs. Perrum had in mind, and I had no wish to find out. I learned all the French verb forms feverishly that night. I had my mother test me on them. I still know the way to conjugate French verbs ending in –*er*, and –*ir*, and –*re*. Fear for one's life is a great motivator.

But I was less successful with Long Division. (It was such a big deal it deserves to be capitalized). I simply didn't get it. It didn't matter what Mrs. Perrum said or did, I could not seem to master it. I would begin the problem and blank out, daydreaming that I was at home alone, watching TV, and holding my stuffed bunny. Then Mrs. Perrum's sharp voice brought me back to reality. I did know enough not to tell her, "I'm stuck." Mrs. Perrum hated to hear that. "What do you mean you're stuck? You don't have any glue on you! So you can't be stuck!" It was permissible to say "I can't do this." With Mrs. Perrum it was crucial to use the right words.

At last, one fine spring day late in the year, I worked a long division problem keeping in mind the formula of divide, multiply, subtract, and bring down. It worked! I will never forget Mrs. Perrum's smile that day. That was the biggest smile the woman ever gave me. It was then that I thought I might not have to remain in fourth grade for the rest of my life. Finally, I reached the end of my fantasy or should I say nightmare that went, "The rest of her classmates grew up and got married. Ann never did. She's still in Mrs. Perrum's class failing at Long Division."

Mrs. Perrum knew how to teach math and she even made the Pythagorean Theorem interesting. I wonder how many people learn the Pythagorean Theorem in fourth grade? "The square of the hypotenuse of a right triangle is equal to the sum of the squares of the other two sides." She drew the diagram and made it colorful with felt markers and a large red and blue "PYTHAGORAS" at the top of the sheet. It was unforgettable. Its supposed purpose in real life is to calculate the shortest route in a road trip, but I prefer Mapquest. Pythagoras did prove useful when I took the standardized GRE math exam for an advanced degree;

it's amazing what a love affair there is between the testing company and Pythagoras.

After the test, I used good old Pythagoras just as much as I've used Algebra in the years after I graduated, which is never. The variable x is of no use in balancing a checkbook. School so often only prepares us for more school. My supposedly less intelligent classmates, who struggled with academics at the time, later proved to be whizzes at basic life and survival skills. I wish I had learned less math and more about how to fix cars and grow food. And after a decade and a half of schooling, it's ludicrous that when my toilet overflows, all I can do is watch in helpless horror.

But some of what I learned that year was sheer fun. Our education included theater. Mrs. Perrum was a skilled pianist and also wrote plays. One was a musical comedy called, *The Yellow Submarine School*. In this play, we were all members of the most senior class in the school. We sang The Beatles' "Yellow Submarine" song and parodied the way our own school was run. We had yellow "school uniforms," which we made during our school art lessons out of crepe paper. Most of us wore yellow, but a few had red, pink, or green costumes. Those girls "got in trouble" with the principal for wearing the wrong colors, just as sometimes happened in real life at our school.

Our class president, a girl named Lucy, played the leading role of the principal, Miss Knowledge. She had glasses like John Lennon (nowadays, Harry Potter) and a brown tweed skirted suit to make her look both wise and a bit like a square (nerd). A girl called "Lily Pink" explained her pink outfit to Miss Knowledge by saying she had received a chemistry set for her birthday and spilled a compound on her dress. "Immediately it all turned pink!" A girl called Rosy Red had on a red outfit because her mother used the wrong detergent. Miss Knowledge then launched into a commercial for New Yellow Zaz Soap Powder that, "…washes dirt OUT and washes yellow IN!" She waved a giant money-saving coupon to encourage us all to buy the soap.

Miss Knowledge pointed out near the end of the play that, "The Top Class has won ALL the cups this year!" and she glowed, "A Truly Remarkable

Achievement!" We ended by singing our School Song, "*Ta-ra-ra Boom-de-ay*." In real life this was a bawdy vaudeville and music hall song written in the 19th century. I was unwittingly being introduced to both high and low culture. Each one of us as "cup winners" got to perform what we were best at, in the school "talent show"—an ingenious way to showcase the talents of everyone in the class to proud parents at the end of the semester.

Although Mrs. Perrum was strict, she taught some fascinating subjects, or at least she made them interesting to her students. She gifted me with her passion for history. We studied Heraldry, the way coats of arms were designed and displayed to symbolize aristocratic family lines. I created and sketched my own "coat of arms" with a keyhole, declaring my father to be a locksmith; the father's trade had to be symbolized. This was a play on my last name which begins with the syllable "Loc." I told the class that I had a cross on my shield shaped like an X. Mrs. Perrum told me sternly that this was not a cross. "Find out what it's called," she commanded.

I picked through several reference books and discovered that an X on a coat of arms was labeled a "saltire." I'm glad I remember it to this day. I would hate to think I wasted all that time.

Mrs. Perrum was a historian *par excellence*. *The Six Wives of Henry the Eighth* became a gripping story of intrigue, treachery, and jostling for power. She read aloud how King Henry wanted to divorce his first wife, Catherine of Aragon, because she was unable to bear him a son and heir to the throne. The Pope, who was in charge of marriage in those days, refused to grant King Henry an annulment. Henry yelled at the Pope, "Shove it!" Well, not exactly.

However, Mrs. Perrum got the message across by pointing out that Henry declared himself the new head of England's church. Then Henry very graciously gave himself permission to get rid of Catherine. The Pope slunk away like a chastised dog, his Pope-tail between his legs.

English history runs with blood. The wives' royal portraits, along with posters of characters from some of Shakespeare's plays, adorned the walls of Mrs. Perrum's classroom. Henry VIII, when not satisfying himself with one of his wives, gorged himself by feasting until he was not only obese, but had multiple health problems. At Hampton Court Palace where he lived, a royal dinner might include a whole ox, six roasted chickens, a dish made of eggs and cream, multiple steaming bowls of potatoes and other vegetables, many bottles of wine and a cheese board. Mrs. Perrum described the gluttonous King Henry's symptoms in minute detail. The king, who was handsome as a young man, in his later years, had a face with tiny eyes sunken under the fat. He had leg ulcers and required a hoist to mount his horse.

Mrs. Perrum also read out loud the wrenching story of Lady Jane Grey, queen for only nine days before she was beheaded. Lady Jane was a pawn in royal politics. Our teacher avowed for us the woman's impassioned plea on the scaffold at the Tower of London as she faced her executioner. "Lady Jane told us that she had never wanted to be queen. Older men, more powerful and ambitious than she, had brought her to this end." The tragedy of it all came through in her tone. When Mrs. Perrum read historical material, I felt as if I was right there.

It was fortunate that I liked history and did well in the subject. Another girl, Tracy Dwight, disliked it and was chronically restless in class. Given the frequency with which she got up and ran around the room she may have had ADHD (an affliction we had not heard of when I was a child). Mrs. Perrum had no patience with Tracy. She found a long piece of twine and tied Tracy to her chair. "I'll tie it loosely," she told Tracy. "Just so when you start to get out of your chair you'll feel it pull and you'll sit down again." The public humiliation was quite enough.

Many years later, Tracy and I connected online through a British school alumni website. Tracy told me, "I hated her for what she put me through. My mother complained to the school and insisted that she be dismissed."

I do not know whether Mrs. Perrum was going to retire anyway or whether she was fired. At any rate, we had a new and less intimidating teacher the following year. Tracy and I both agreed that were it not for the lack of opportunities for working women in the late 1960s in England, Mrs. Perrum probably would have been a university professor. She had little patience for the normal behavior of fourth graders.

I found out that year that someone whom initially I prayed never to have contact with turned out to be someone who was familiar with bawdy vaudeville songs such as those performed by Gilbert and Sullivan; who was as much of a Beatles fan as I was; who understood parody and appreciated all types of comedy. My most vivid memory of her is on our last day of class when she read an actual advertisement in the newspaper that someone had placed to sell a musical instrument. "Piano for sale by lady with four mahogany legs!"

48

FIFTH GRADE, TOP CLASS AT NORLAND PLACE

Norland Place had all kinds of quirks, such as main dishes and desserts that consisted of pure starch. Baked beans on toast and spaghetti on toast were staples in British children's tea. (Tea was a meal, of course, not just a drink). At school we had rice pudding, bread pudding, semolina, and of course lots of custard. British schools had the peculiar notion, dating from Queen Victoria's time, that eating poorly-made bland milk puddings built character. The school also had "water" listed on the school menu as part of the meal. Once we finished eating our puddings and drinking our water, we had gym class. Our gym teacher would shepherd us in groups from one apparatus to another in an almost military manner. I can still hear Mrs. Moore's voice barking, "Ropes to the bar, bar to the box, box to the mats, mats to the ropes!" We hustled to comply, moving swiftly from one apparatus to another.

On Monday, we had Games, which was not as much fun as it sounds. We played Rounders, the British girls' version of softball, and Netball, the British girls' version of basketball. I had no talent at either one. Are all writers bad at athletics? I am sure a few people are talented at writing and sports, but for the most part, it seems to be one or the other. I was always a decent writer but it seemed to carry the penalty of me being hopeless at physical endeavors of any type.

Just like when I attended Dusseldorf Primary, I was the last one to be picked for any team. I wonder if schools still engage in the brutal

Darwinian practice of choosing up sides? It was a daily reminder of one's athletic skill and popularity... or lack thereof.

I always knew who would be chosen first, and I was always left standing alone when everyone else had joined their group. Later, as a teenager, I sang with gusto Janis Ian's song 'At Seventeen' where she remembers, "For those whose names were never called, when choosing sides for basketball." She could have been singing right to me. We went for games in a motor coach from school to the vast grounds of Wormwood Scrubs Prison, where "The Games" were played. Possibly our headmistress got cheap rent there.

When games or gym ended, I was finally able to feel some sense of relief. In English class I read *Jane Eyre* and entered the world of the Bronte sisters. My teacher, Mrs. Philippa Lucas, was a feminist, as was Charlotte Bronte all those years ago. For a homework assignment I learned from an encyclopedia, that Charlotte, Emily, and Anne Bronte had submitted their manuscripts for publication using the men's names of Currer, Ellis, and Acton Bell. If they had used their own female names, they would not have been published. Mrs. Lucas talked often of how "Victorian England was a man's world."

As a divorced woman, teaching more than three decades ago, she may have been referring to her own life, as well. There was plenty for women to complain about in 1970s England. Philippa Lucas was about forty, with dark brown wavy hair streaked with gray, and almost black eyes. She wore miniskirts, which were fashionable then. She had a daughter our age. We knew she smoked because she smelled of it and had a raspy voice and prematurely wrinkled skin. She once dropped her cigarettes, and I picked them up for her. But she was never seen smoking; it wouldn't have been proper. She came to school on the London Underground, carrying a wicker basket that contained her tiny Yorkshire terrier, Pip, named for the character in Charles Dickens's novel *Great Expectations*. We read that, too.

I wrote poetry in Mrs. Lucas's classes, my first stab at doing so. I wrote about a little girl named Angela.

Angela was the queerest child,
She wasn't meek and she wasn't mild.
All she wanted to do was sit,
In her chair and have a fit!

My elders must have laughed. I did win an essay contest at the school, though, and was proud to receive a silver trophy for a story featuring the Greek gods and goddesses whose myths I had devoured. In my story, I had Zeus and Ariadne and Dionysus, with a few magical fairies thrown in for good measure. One of the fairies ended up marrying Prometheus, who in Greek myth is a major figure and an all-around important dude. Even today, I enjoy putting disparate people together in stories to create something new.

Later, I found out that Philippa Lucas had been a mentor and role model for many other teachers at Norland Place. She planted the seeds for my later feminism. She also did something less useful; she taught my classmates and me a word I came to hate. During an English class on "Colloquialisms" we learned about expressions such as "a skeleton in the closet" and, "hoist on your own petard." One of the colloquialisms on the list was "a goody-goody." Mrs. Lucas told us that this was someone who obsessively kept the rules and was almost too good to be true.

My arch-enemy in that class, Aimee, said, "Oh, like Ann Lee." From that day until the end of the year I was subjected to the singsong jeer, "Ann Lee's a Goody-Goody!"

Despite my teacher setting me up for taunting, I always liked her. But I did not realize until later how good she was. Life is often like that. Gratitude comes in hindsight.

We had studied the Tudors under Mrs. Perrum. We looked at the Stuarts with Mrs. Lucas. It wasn't as exciting with Mrs. Lucas, but I enjoyed her more relaxed approach. We created two posters comparing Stuart England with the present. We depicted scenes from Charles II's reign with women in long dresses and horses and carts in the streets with scenes from

Queen Elizabeth's modern England with its 1970s disco, schoolgirls playing hockey, and a photo of the nearby Notting Hill Gate shopping street. We voted to call the display "What a Difference!" Although I wish we had followed a classmate's suggestion that we use the king and queen's names in a jazzy way and call our posters "Charlie and Lizzie." Mrs. Lucas did not think that was respectful, although she laughed.

There was a girl in my class whom I'll call "Sheila." Sheila was the ultimate misfit. Her father was a titled Lord, called Lord Mitchell. Sheila often reminded us that when he died, she would be The Honorable Sheila Mitchell. She was fat, wore round glasses, and had mousy brown hair. She liked fashion designing, and drew weird clothes. We told her how strange we thought they were. She brought women's magazines to school to seem grown up. We took one of them away from her and played "keep away" with it. When Sheila would get near the person holding the magazine, that person threw it to someone else. This went on until class started. I still remember Sheila's tear-stained face as she howled to Mrs. Lucas, "They took my Woman's Own! Oh, Mrs. Lucas, they're being *very unkind* to me!"

Then there was the day the chalkboard came off the wall. The top two nails somehow came loose, so the base of the board remained sitting on the ledge, but the top of the board came down and hit her on the head, releasing a cloud of chalk dust. We gasped. Then we giggled. It was Sheila after all; if it had happened to someone more popular we would not have laughed. Today I know that I owe Sheila thanks. She was teased, which allowed that I sometimes went unscathed. I hope she overcame what we did to her, and I hope she's living well.

The girl everyone loved and whose company we all craved was named Vivien. Vivien had long silver-blond hair and blue eyes. Her parents were rich. She was smart. In fourth grade, I remember the teacher announcing after asking a question and soliciting answers, "Vivien is the only one who got it right."

Vivien was athletic. She was funny. She could also put someone down in an instant. If someone made a gross joke, Vivien would raise her eyebrows, roll her eyes, and say in a long drawn out upper class voice, "That is ABsolutely reVOLting." She lived on an exclusive street in London called Linden Gardens. We copied everything Vivien did. When she collected the free books offered in the girls' comic book *Mandy,* we all tried to get them too. Vivien showed off these two booklets. *The Forget Me Not Book* for addresses and *The Forget Me Not Book* for autographs were both covered with small, beautiful blue flowers. Just the fact that Vivien had them made them Highly Desirable Items.

I had the misfortune of buying the wrong comic book those two weeks and cried at my missed opportunity. Some might think this a trivial matter, but a child's world is small and little things are a big deal. When Vivien brought potato chips to school to eat at break time, we all asked our mothers to buy them for us as well.

Vivien left Norland Place to attend Roedean, the most expensive and elite boarding school in England. She later owned her own business. Vivien was one of those people who would always do well in life. Like my brother, she seemed to have been born under a lucky star.

49

A LOSS OF INNOCENCE

W hen not at school, my sister and I and the other children in our apartment building played in Ladbroke Square, a private gated park around the corner. We had to join a club, subscribe, and pay a fee to receive two of their much-coveted gate keys. Ladbroke Square was where we endlessly played Spies. James Bond 007 was our hero, and we spent many a weekend afternoon outwitting the Russians, otherwise known as the kids who lived on the other side of the Square.

Ladbroke Square was also where I met Mr. Donnelly. Mom was getting on my case for being so deathly shy, so I was determined to practice being friendly with this stranger, his wife, and twelve-year-old daughter. Mr. Donnelly was overweight, but seemed nice. He guessed my age as "eight or nine," and as I was almost nine, I thought he was very clever to figure this out. When I saw him and his family walking around the park I would stop and chat.

One day, Mr. Donnelly was playing tennis with another man, and his family was not with him. I was passing by when his partner hit a shot wild. I ran to chase the ball since it landed near me. I brought it back and handed it to a sweaty Mr. Donnelly. He said, "That was a big help. I'm going to give you a big kiss for that."

I looked at the fat sweaty man, wrinkled my nose, and said, "No thank you."

"No thank you?" answered Mr. Donnelly. "Whaddya mean? Well, I'll catch you and do it!"

I ran, but he was too fast for me. He grabbed me and gave me a wet, slobbery kiss on the lips. "Thank you for getting the ball."

When I told my mother what Mr. Donnelly had done, she said, "I don't really think it's fair for an adult to kiss a child like that." Other than saying this, she did nothing. I learned that there was nothing one could do about such matters. Other than that one time, I was never sexually abused, but Mr. Donnelly taught me that day that the possibility was there. Some might quibble over calling this sexual abuse, but the best definition I have heard of sexual abuse is when someone touches me and instead of feeling like something is being given to me, it feels like something is being taken away from me. That is exactly how I felt.

Mr. Donnelly also taught me that men bigger and stronger than me could use force to get what they want from me. Good luck might protect me. Or not. I learned that day that my boundaries would not be respected and that my body was not my own. A decade later, I was wondering out loud to a friend if what had happened to me was sexual abuse. "Of course it was," she responded. "He raped your lips."

It was a relief in my thirties to realize I'd been a lesbian all along. Once I started seeing women, I had no more worries about date rape. One of the less appreciated aspects of my sexual orientation is that it's safer than being straight; about one woman in every five in this country is sexually assaulted. I'm not saying that this is why women are lesbians; for me, being a lesbian is like being left-handed. I was born with both.

50

NO, I WASN'T SPARED MIDDLE SCHOOL

At the age of eleven, after having passed the state examination with high grades, I went to secondary school. Middle and high school were combined at the prestigious Godolphin and Latymer Girls' School. What I most remember about it was that instead of walking, I took the bus because it was further away. I remember getting off the bus, getting closer to the school, and seeing the stone buildings and blank black windows looming larger and larger as my feet crunched the gravel driveway past the black wrought-iron gates. I never failed to check my watch at the front gate to be sure I was early or on time. Being late meant facing a teacher who announced in the voice of judgment, in front of the entire class, that you would be in detention the following day. That may be why I'm compulsively early to so many events even today.

When exams were given, we were expected to "revise" the year's work in preparation, but no direct instruction in study skills was offered. On exam day, it was sink or swim. There were four grades: Excellent, Good, Low but passing, and Fail. Girls who received the letter F, meant they had "fucked-up," which the more uncouth girls admitted. Results were read out to the entire class. In sixth grade biology and seventh grade English, our class heard, "Ann Locasio: Fail!"

I had fallen so far since the days of Mrs. Perrum and Mrs. Lucas.

Lunch was a time to catch one's breath and briefly escape the relentless pressure to perform. In sixth grade, I sat at Table 17. There was a rotation chart on the wall. One did not line up for food until the table number was called. Attendance was also taken by number, with class members counting off. I was number 19. It was crucially important not to forget your number. It would be unthinkable to have the mind wander after number 18 was called and not immediately shout "Nineteen!" However, you had to be sure that the person in front was completely finished saying "Eighteen" so both numbers would be heard. If you held up the process, everyone would laugh at you.

Bad homework was displayed for all to see. One day, we all sat at our old wooden desks in room 204. The floorboards creaked as Mrs. Samuels, the grey-haired history teacher with body odor who smelled like stale cigarettes, walked toward me. She was smiling as she held up my poorly done map of Renaissance Europe. She pointed out how I had not followed instructions, and had skimped on details. She walked the notebook up and down all three aisles, to make sure everyone could view it and know that this was what they should not do. She took her time, so as not to miss anyone. The entire time she was pointing out all the faults in the assignment, she kept smiling.

After Mrs. Samuels had dismissed us and I went home, I got a knife and cut myself. The pain provided a strange relief. I didn't mind the blood, although I put on a long-sleeved shirt to make sure my mother never saw it. I was afraid if she saw my arms she would make me repeat what had happened when I was eight years old and got extra math assignments from a psychologist as punishment.

I found some relief from school in my Saturday morning judo lessons. I had my first exposure to martial arts at the age of twelve in 1972. It helped me work out some of my experiences with middle school. Doing the intense calisthenics required, followed by learning how to throw each other in the class was major physical exercise. I was eager to show off a judo throw in the early days of class, and Lisa agreed to let me demonstrate on her. I started by saying, "Stand opposite me with your legs slightly apart and bend your knees."

Lisa broke up laughing. "So when there's a burglar in your house you're going to come up to him and say, 'I want to throw you to the ground, so stand there with my money, bend your knees, and spread your legs wider?'"

I kept up the judo lessons, dreaming of the day I would throw Lisa to the ground. I received a label-maker for my birthday that year. Now able to make what I considered professional looking sticky labels, I stuck them on everything. On the shade of the desk lamp in my bedroom, I had a label that read, "Do Judo. Keep Fit."

Lisa sneaked into my bedroom and "borrowed" my label maker. When I returned, under my label was another one that read, "Don't Do Judo. It's Shit."

I knew she was trying to get me worked up, but on this occasion she didn't succeed. I answered with another label: "Do Judo. Your Pants Won't Split."

Lisa's next label read, "If They Do, Don't Sit."

51
CHALLENGES AND CRISES

On the trip back to London from the United States in 1971, we were met by my father's company chauffeur, Mr. Cousins. He offered us candy. It tasted terrible. I knew I was back to difficult reality and the return to British school. Goodbye heavenly Hershey's chocolate kisses, hello disgusting English boiled "sweeties." Strange, how so many early memories in one way or another relate to food. Sugar, again.

When school started, I was required to make a dress in Domestic Science (Home Ec) class with Mrs. Bird. Mrs. Bird was the sort of ultra-practical person who found me incomprehensible. My love of fairy tales and creative writing were of no use in the precise world of sewing. I knew exactly how Anne of Green Gables must have felt when she had to sew patchwork. When Mrs. Bird instructed us to "alter our dress patterns," I had no idea what she was talking about. I still don't, but it's too late to ask now. Ruefully, I recall asking stupid questions and needing help with the most elementary stitches, which resulted in crooked hems. I never even learned how to thread the electric sewing machine. To this day when I see a Hobby Lobby I break out in hives.

I'm so glad I attended Godolphin and Latymer in the 1970s. It gives me reason to get up each day now and be thankful that I will never have to go there again. I got off the bus in the London district of Hammersmith, which I recall as having dark, forbidding row houses with nobody going in or out of them. The weather, in my memory, is always the same—darkly overcast. It's raining or it's about to. The wind gusts, and tattered sheets of stray newspaper and dead leaves whirl into the side of the curb. I would walk to school in my uniform gray raincoat with a scarlet lined hood. One time I walked with a girl named Julia who spent the entire journey to school telling me about another girl who didn't like me, and giving me all the reasons why.

We approached the tall black gates and the brown school buildings with windows I couldn't see into. Gravel crunched under my feet. I came in out of the cold to the falsely comforting warmth of the cloakroom where our lockers were located, which were actually see-through hanging baskets. Their transparency was to prevent girls from hiding drugs there.

Nothing was hidden, including how messy my locker was. Godolphin and Latymer was a place of ironclad restraint. I remember having to hold in the surging energy in my eleven-year-old body to conform to the "No Running" rule. We were expected to have the decorum of middle-aged ladies. But that has now changed. Now that I'm a middle-aged lady, I have the decorum of an eleven-year-old. I have to make up for what I lost.

Homework was collected in piles in front of our classroom to be graded, in my case, usually with comments like "Deficient" and "Do Over" and a constant "Improve Your Handwriting." I never did. Thank god for keyboarding.

Fortunately, I had playful and immature peers, sitting near me in the sixth grade classroom, to take the edge off. We passed notes during Miss Thomson's math lessons, especially when she taught the units on symmetry, sines and cosines, and vectors. For some reason, I stopped passing notes when we covered statistics and probability. The odds of winning the lottery seemed eternally interesting. It's also comforting now to have a statistical background when everyone panics over airline crashes and terrorist attacks, knowing that the probability of experiencing either one is infinitesimal. I shake my head in disbelief at those fearful of these events—the same people who refuse to buckle their seat belts or get a flu shot.

What I did not realize until later was that many of my peers were as scared at school as I was. We took some small comfort in each other. We invented secret languages to try to hide our impolite and honest speech from the teachers. I remember Ucka-Ucka Language, where one said a consonant followed by Ucka, and vowels were Acka, Ecka, Icka, Ocka, and Ucka. In between each word we said Tug. So, for example, "yes" would be Yucka Ecka Sucka Tug. For obvious reasons, F was Ficka. I was tremendously proud of how clever we were. Only later did I find that our American cousins, including Cousin Mark, had done the same thing two years earlier with their own secret "Alfa-Alfa" language. I am not sure how it worked except that "shit" became "shilfitty." And even my friends' parents spoke Pig Latin.

I got my first chain letter that year, too. I truly believed I would receive 312 pounds and 50 pence in English money—about $500 at the 1970 exchange rate—if I made five copies of the letter and shared it with friends. I gladly sent ten pence to my classmate, Suzanne Shute, who was at the top of the list. Instead of receiving $500 I obtained an important life lesson and lost ten pence. Suzanne is a doctor now. Perhaps she'll pay me back.

Godolphin and Latymer did give me the chance to play Quince in the play, *A Midsummer Night's Dream*, on Shakespeare Day. We had an entire day where the whole school, by class, put on a play by Shakespeare. As Quince, I played a country yokel with stage fright who was to introduce my fellow yokels who were going to perform for Duke Theseus of Athens and his wife, the Lady Hippolyta—a play within a play.

I came forward in my dirty shirt and breeches and began to speak to my classmates who were playing the Duke and his Lady:

> "If we offend, it is w-w-with our good
> will, That you should think, W-w-we
> come not to offend, but with good
> will, to show our simple skill, That is
> the t-t-t-true beginning of our end."

If this seems not to make sense, it doesn't. Shakespeare didn't intend it to. The stage fright was real, too. The stern history teacher who held up my homework as a bad example, and the teacher who had loudly announced my exam failures to the class, were watching and scowling. But that worked in my favor. Frightened old Quince, trembling and shaking, came to life in me. It was my proudest moment that year.

Our entire class got into trouble the day that someone made a piece of poster board and hung it on the wall during lunch hour. It said, "Mary had a little lamb, she also had a duck. She put them on the mantelpiece, to see if they would F…all off!" Our instructors were not amused. Nor were they impressed when someone sneaked into the school library and replaced the shelf titles of such headlines as "Fiction" and "History" and "Science" with "Shit Here" and "Eric's Got a Hernia."

The girls who did it may have gotten the idea from a boys' school prankster who had rearranged similar plastic letters to read "Dr. Jack Offalott."

52

MY GIFTED PEERS

I n order to be admitted to Godolphin and Latymer, a girl had to be the
best, not only when it came to getting top grades on the state exam called
the Eleven-Plus, during an interview process. The interviews were con-
ducted by several teachers in several different rooms where math and English
skills were assessed. Afterwards, fifty percent of us were accepted and the
other half rejected. No wonder my peers were dazzlingly clever. G & L, as
we called our school, was bedecked with brilliance. Me, I was in the bottom
quarter. I never realized that I had done well just to be admitted there. The
whole time I was there, I was convinced that I was not all that smart.

The class I most dreaded was French with Miss Dawson. The class
combined the teacher who seemed to hate me most with some of the
meanest girls in my age group. Miss Dawson played favorites, and because
I was the worst in the class, I was not one of them. Mostly, I just watched
as Karina, who was both beautiful and great at French, charmed Miss
Dawson. Miss Dawson, when she was not teaching, loved Steve McQueen
and watched all his movies. I always hoped that when she entered the classroom, she had seen a new Steve McQueen film as she would talk about it at
some length, sparing me some minutes of work time.

One afternoon, Karina marched up to Miss Dawson's desk. Karina,
with her long curly brown hair and generous eyelashes, could get away
with marching to a teacher's desk at random. She presented Miss Dawson

with a Steve McQueen poster. Then she recited a poem she had written which began, "Through this whole year, we have seen… That you dream of Steve McQueen." Miss Dawson was charmed, and she laughed and clapped as she unrolled the glossy poster on which the poem was written, delaying the start of the lesson for ten minutes. Behind Miss Dawson's back, Karina made excellent jokes about farting, and I learned a lot that year about the power of humor to help a kid get away with stuff.

Being in that class for a year and a half left its mark. I still sometimes flash back to Miss Dawson calling on me out of the blue when I was dissociating because I didn't understand her rapid-fire French. "ANN LO-CA-SI-O!" she thundered. I could never answer and after a few of the longest moments ever, she would give a self-satisfied smirk and ask for a volunteer.

However, these days when I have insomnia, I pretend that I'm asleep in her class behind a screen where nobody can see me and she cannot call on me. I feel safe and slumber soon comes.

Miss Dawson now lives on in permanent memory at the school as she eventually endowed the school with a French prize for a graduating senior. That's all right. It taught me that the wicked sometimes prosper. There's nothing I can do about it, and living well is the best revenge.

Not all the teachers were this brutal, although a surprising number of them were. Just remember that I was a sensitive child, and that school was not the right place for me. Fortunately, Miss Toller arrived in my second year. She was the music teacher who replaced the meanest music teacher I have ever encountered. Mrs. Evans, her predecessor, asked all of us to draw pictures of all the stringed musical instruments. As always, my hand shook as I drew them. Mrs. Evans gave my assignment back to me with a "D," and declared to the class, "These instruments look like they've been in a car crash."

When I auditioned for the Junior Choir, she told me I had no talent and would never be allowed in.

Miss Toller, in contrast, gave me the chance to sing in the Junior Choir and also the Christmas Carols Choir. I remember feeling enormous pride when I entered the hall for the school Christmas concert and saw both my parents sitting there. Miss Toller played guitar and taught us contemporary Christian songs such as, "Lord of the Dance" and selections from *Joseph and His Coat of Many Colors*, which were catchy and easy to sing. She was good-natured, so when we placed a plastic dog turd in her desk wrapped in a pair of underpants, she laughed and took it well.

I was secretly pleased when Sarah and Olivia, the most daring and rebellious girls in school, marched off to the Pupil Power demonstration held in Trafalgar Square in 1972. I recall the thrill of seeing their picture in the daily paper in full school uniform, smoking cigarettes. I wonder to this day how many detentions they received. They did us all a favor though. Later that year, the school got its first Student Council. They called it the "School Forum," and with Miss Toller's encouragement I represented my class there, articulating the concerns that other girls relayed to me.

The school's older girls also set up a free-speech event in the school courtyard where any girl could get up on the wooden box provided and say whatever was on her mind. Their soapbox was a schoolgirls' version of the Speaker's Corner at Hyde Park, where anyone could get up and make a speech on anything, from the sublime to the ridiculous. We loved our soapbox sessions. The most popular topic I remember was "All Homework Should Be Abolished!"

The decision of the school administration to let the girls express themselves more freely was a wise move. It defused some of the built-up resentment from not having our concerns heard.

A suggestion box also got nailed to the wall outside the assembly hall. And we acquired a bulletin board to trade items, find homes for pets, and sell our posters of David Cassidy and Donny Osmond. Evidently, I was not the only unhappy one at the school at that time. From what I can ascertain, the school is a far different place now since it became independent instead of being a state-supported school, with parents as paying customers. Funny how that works. But at least it looks happy and vibrant on its website, while maintaining its long held standards of scholarly and athletic excellence.

Despite my secondary school's challenges, it did me one favor for which I shall be eternally grateful. When the King Tutankhamen Exhibition came to the London Museum, we went there on a school field trip. We got off the red double-decker London bus and walked to the museum. The line went around a full city block. As we were pre-booked, we marched right in. There, an impressionable twelve-year-old witnessed King Tut's tiny wooden toy chariot, as perfectly preserved as the day it was buried with him. His gold mask, vividly highlighted and striped with blue, was unstained and unsullied. I did not realize then that I had been given the experience of a lifetime. It left me with a love of Egyptian history that continues to this day.

The most inspiring educator I had at Godolphin and Latymer was Miss G. Shepherd. It was strictly forbidden for us to know teachers' first names. As there were two Miss Shepherds, one was Miss A. Shepherd and the other Miss G. Shepherd. Miss A. Shepherd taught math and rumor had it she failed half her class on the end-of-year exams. Miss G. Shepherd, on the other hand, was young and had creative ideas for our English class activities. We once took turns going to the front of the class to teach each other something. It could be anything at all: how to throw an egg; how to eat pie; how to doodle.

Or, we had "three minute speeches" where we had to talk on an assigned topic for three minutes without saying "Um" or pausing longer than three seconds, or repeating any word other than an article. The audience could call us out on any of these missteps by yelling, "hesitation!" or "repetition!" or "Um!" Sometimes we acted out spoofed TV ads for "Spazz Laundry Detergent" or "Brush-ee-Doodle Toothpaste," which were our attempts at mocking consumerism.

We also played Yes and No, where people asked us yes or no questions, but we were not allowed to answer with those two words. If I was in the hot seat and someone asked, "Are you feeling hot?" I would have to say, "I am not currently feeling that way" or something similar. We also had dramatic exercises. We had to enact a made-up "Primitive Ritual" where we could speak, but it had to be a fake language. The meaning of the ritual had to be conveyed in actions. Our group did "The Uniting of All Brothers and Sisters," with ritualized somersaults and a silent language of facial grimaces and tongues poking out.

On April Fool's Day, we all turned our desks so they were facing the back of the room before English class. When Miss G. Shepherd came in, we all faced the other way. She wasn't fazed. She walked to the back of the room, looked at us, and said, "Today we're having an extremely horrible Spelling Test." One of the spelling words was "*Recumbolesque*." As I can't find that word on Dictionary.com, Miss G. Shepherd either made it up or it has fallen into disuse.

We also had frequent debates. In the British style, each debate had a theme that started, "This house believes that…" One person would take the side of the "house," while the other argued against that position. We had spirited arguments on "This house believes that abortion is murder," and "This house believes that the only course a rational human being can follow is that of complete self-interest," and "This house believes that labor strikes should be prohibited."

A more whimsical topic was, "This house believes that brains are more important than beauty." A very lovely girl named Polly, with long, curly blond hair, predictably took the opposing side. I can still see her tossing her long curls so that they cascaded down her back. "It's *obvious*," she purred to us, "that it's best to be *beauuuuutiful*. I mean, look at Perdita and Jessica over there."

Perdita and Jessica were two of Polly's best friends, but although they were brilliant and popular, they did not have Polly's long, lush golden hair, deep blue eyes, or rosy cheeks. Perdita had ramrod-straight brown hair and a snub nose with freckles. Jessica's nickname was "Budgie" because people said she looked like the British bird called a budgerigar. "Poor Perdita and Jessica!" lamented Polly. "Such *nice* people, but aren't they a *sorry* sight to behold!"

I learned from this that even when it seems that there is one obvious right side of an argument, it is possible to produce the other side convincingly. Polly, I saw, had some truth on her side. She got away with misbehavior because she was so charming, beautiful, and funny.

Academic research has since shown that attractive people are indeed considered more intelligent and capable. I am sure that Polly, so smart as well as so attractive, is highly successful these days. Perhaps her skill at seeing both sides of an argument made her into a good lawyer.

Perdita, her friend, was no slouch though. She seemed to absorb Polly's teasing good-naturedly. Later, when it came time for Perdita to do her fake TV commercial in English class, she upstaged Polly's beauty-enhancing cosmetic ads by inventing a new tampon. "This is the new improved tampon 'Sprunge,'" she announced. "It comes in three ways. Regular, for a light flow. Or Plus, for your more, uh, difficult days. And Super Plus. That's for a torrent."

53

MISCHIEF WITH MARVELOUS MO

My sister had by now left Norland Place to go to her own secondary school. It was a friendly private school called Francis Holland. Lisa's best friend there was a girl with Greek parents. Her name was Violando Goulandris. Her millionaire father owned a fleet of cargo ships. When Violando was born as the fourth child in her family, an uncle quoted a TV show popular at the time and said, "She's the last of the Mohicans." Because of that statement, she was nicknamed Mo. When Mo came to spend a Saturday night, anything might happen. Mo and my sister once visited a joke shop and bought a stink bomb. It was a transparent, thin plastic egg with liquid inside it. They broke it open in a London bus. Immediately, people started saying, "Oy! Who farted? Was it you? Was it you?" At the next stop, everyone got off and the bus came to a standstill.

We always had a midnight feast when Mo stayed over. We set an alarm, and at midnight we would pull out our hidden stash of candy, bought earlier in the day. Lisa would provide song and dance for entertainment. Mo told jokes. At "dark-thirty" in the morning any joke is funny.

The next morning we visited the photo booth at the nearby shopping center. We took turns running in and out of the booth for solo pictures, then we all piled in for the last shot. We also played Consequences, a game which involved writing story lines on a piece of paper, folding it over to hide them, and passing the paper to the next person. The end result might be, "Hankley met Mo in a public toilet where they explored each other's bodies. He said to her, 'Your breasts are as big as hot air balloons.' She said to him, 'Don't exaggerate so much.' Because of this, the Prime Minister's pants fell down." The story always ended, "Because of this…" hence the name Consequences. I remember peals of laughter playing Consequences.

At Mo's house, we played Big Business. We were all businessmen, and I do mean men. There were few females in business at that time and we did not know any of them. Mo took the name of Lord J. Brundleberry, Lisa was the CEO of the firm Lovebird and Killjoy, and I was Mr. Montague-Padgett. Mo's house was ideal for playing Big Business as every room had an intercom system, and several rooms had trays mounted to the wall to leave notes for other family members or servants. So when Lord J. Brundleberry wrote up an invoice to deliver "100 Tons of Crow's Vomit" to Mr. Lovebird of Lovebird and Killjoy, Inc., it occasioned much running up and down stairs, leaving "documents" for the other to pick up, and unending giggles.

Mo was also a good mimic. She imitated the stupidest girl in school— Julia. The chemistry teacher had asked her, "Julia, what is delivery tubing used for?" Mo, feigning a vacant look in her wide brown eyes, answered, "Deliveries?"

It didn't matter what we did, Mo could make anything fun. One time Mo, Lisa, and I were looking at my brother Hankley's baby book, which nobody had bothered to update in years. We got to a blank page where a parent could record, "Mental Development." Mo chortled. "Look! The child is ten years old. Nothing yet."

One weekend, when Mo stayed over, we pooled our allowances to buy "porn" at the local newsstand. The local newsstand sold newspapers, magazines, cigarettes, and candy. The so-called porn we wanted to buy was nothing like *Playboy* or *Hustler*. It was a comic book of crude sex jokes and cartoons called *Funny Half Hour*. A person was supposed to be at least 14 years old to buy it, but my sister walked confidently up to the clerk's counter and asked for one. She was given it with no questions asked. I learned then that if a person acts like she knows what she's doing, she often gets away with it; it's those who look unsure of themselves who are questioned.

Lisa scored status points with Mo at school the next week for her daring. We hustled out of the newspaper shop with our illicit magazine in hand, and went into Ladbroke Square Gardens to devour it. It was a thick magazine so we sat down on a park bench near the rose garden, pulled up the staples and divided the magazine into three parts. As we read and gasped and giggled, who should come along but old Mrs. Cohen.

Mrs. Cohen had rigid ideas of what children should and should not be doing, and reading *Funny Half Hour* would not have earned her approval, but would have earned her telling our parents. As she drew closer to us, in unison we all sat on our respective one-third of the magazine, crossed our legs like young ladies, folded our hands, and chorused, "Good morning, Mrs. Cohen."

Mrs. Cohen had her elderly gray poodle Mitzi with her and was forever chiding her pet. "Oh, Mitzi darling, don't do that. Mitzi darling, walk to heel. Mitzi darling, don't snap." Mitzi sometimes bit people.

Mrs. Cohen had stringy salt and pepper gray hair, red pimples all over her face and beady black eyes that perpetually darted around her as she looked for misbehaving children. She was the same woman who yelled at us for playing outside her window at our apartment building. My father said that she sat at home reprimanding her dog and picking at her cheeks, so the acne never healed. Her insistence on children never being noisy and on overall flawless good conduct was ironic given that her husband, Bernard, produced pornographic movies. He had just put out a film called *Baby Love* using the song by the same title sung by The Supremes. If we had known that at the time, we could have shared our *Funny Half Hour* with Pauline Cohen and offered her pointers for Bernard's next movie.

Mo made gentle fun of her other friend Caroline Keesh. Caroline was sweet but not the brightest button in the bag. She would call Mo on some evenings to take a break from homework and say, "Mo! I have this new record. It's such *lovely* music. Let me put it on and play it for you. I'll hold the phone near the record player so you can sing along."

Mo said it was a long song and she got really bored listening to all the verses, but she allowed Caroline to do it. Mo was funny, but she was also kind. She did not make fun of people publicly at their expense. She did tell us, after recounting the story of Caroline Keesh's long song, that she expected her to call again another day. She said, "Next time Caroline will probably say, 'I'm mixing a cake right now using a new recipe and I want you to try it. I'll pour it down the phone!'"

Mo was also astutely observant. She noted to us, "Whenever policemen come to the school to give their road safety lecture, all the teachers start flirting. I mean, it's a girls' school, and suddenly there's this MAN! Miss Jones, our English teacher, is normally so-o-o proper, but when young, dark-haired, good-looking P.C. Prendergast showed up, she stood up straight, fluttered her eyelashes, and puffed out her boobs." Mo gave an imitation of young Miss Jones, fluffing up her hair to add to the effect.

54

ALTERNATE REALITY: MONTY PYTHON

Guilt tripper: *Drink your coffee! There are people sleeping in India!*

For comic relief I had not only Mo, but also Monty Python. Monty Python was my middle school sanity saver. These men presented theater of the absurd, and were my introduction to satire. I fell in love with satire then and there, and remained smitten. I adored the Dead Parrot Sketch and the Cheese Shop, but gave top honors to the Argument Clinic, which I consider their best work. It was a joyous day when I saved enough money to buy Monty Python's Big Red Book, which was of course blue. I no longer have it, but I remember its bizarre graphics of policemen with breasts and strange frog-like creatures snuggled up to naked people next to their genitalia.

Juvenile, yes, but brilliant too. There was the Children's Page where a kindly old storekeeper ran a quaint little shop selling…contraceptives. Next to this were lots of Xs indicating deletion of X-rated material with the occasional reference to nakedness amidst all the obliterations. The page was decorated with cartoonish dancing bunnies which added to the effect. The book's Australian Page was, of course, upside down.

In the midst of all the giggles there were lessons: Much of life is absurd and doesn't make sense, people can be jerks for no reason, all human societies have strange and arbitrary rules, and to improve your standing among your friends, learn how to do the *Silly Walk*. I've heard that John Cleese flatly refuses to do the *Silly Walk*. Possibly being as tall as he is, he may have back problems which preclude it. Or maybe he's sick and tired of being asked.

I was lucky as a teenager to be educated by Monty Python. I am quite serious. My developing adolescent brain devoured the satire of these Cambridge-educated young men. I memorized entire sketches, not knowing that years later, I would recite those lines with my friends, live and on Facebook. "This is an ex-parrot!" I would cry. In a scene from a bookstore Mark Cleese plays the customer and asks, "Can I buy the book called *Great Expectations*? Great is spelled G-R-A-T-E." From *Monty Python and the Holy Grail*, Cleese threatens, "I am going to fart in your general direction," which was, decades later, used as a line of satire in a political protest march to make fun of the adversary.

One of the Pythons disputed the legitimacy of King Arthur becoming king because he extracted a sword from a stone with the help of an aquatic nymph. "Do you really think you should be king just because some watery tart threw a sword at you?"

And there was the line we quoted endlessly at school after anything surprising happened, "Nobody expects the Spanish Inquisition!"

For those familiar with Monty Python, heads will nod. Others may wonder what on earth I'm talking about. Look it up. You'll be glad you did.

Monty Python got me through Godolphin and Latymer. In English classes the cool girls reenacted their sketches, as people around the world were soon to do. In the 1960s the youth had The Beatles for music, but in the 1970s we had Monty Python for comedy. I got both as I was on the tail end of The Beatles, but it is for the Pythons that I am the most thankful. So now I'm going to throw verbal bouquets to all of them. John Cleese, Eric Idle, Terry Jones, Terry Gilliam, Michael Palin, and Graham Chapman, who died much too soon…I love you guys forever.

It's just as well that I had the Pythons, because so much of British TV back then was desperately bad. Special mention must be made of BBC 2 in those days. BBC 1 had all the good shows, and BBC 2 was there to make BBC 1 look good. One had to work hard to be that awful. For most of the day, BBC 2 did not even broadcast. There was a test pattern of a rather ugly young girl with long, lifeless brown hair surrounded by a patchwork of garish colors and perpetual Muzak playing the same songs over and over.

When dusk fell, the test pattern at last faded, so that once a week we watched the evening program, which announced, "Live from Birmingham, it's the Golden Shot!" This was a game show that had a camera looking through a metal viewing circle at a target and the player had to say, "Go right" "left" "up a little" "No, down again" and then "Fire!" A miniature missile shot out and zoomed at the goal. Except for once, when a gloriously stupid man was playing, contestants unfailingly hit the target. It depended on laboriously making sure the viewing circle completely surrounded the light bulb that the player was trying to hit. There was no time limit, so sometimes people took several minutes to position the viewer for firing. Once they hit their mark, the host spent another five minutes praising the contestant for aiming well. I wonder how the show ever stayed on the air. I suspect that it was only because the government paid for it and there were no Nielsen ratings.

Then there was Going for a Song, the first feeble attempt at an Antiques Roadshow. I remember one episode with a middle-aged woman named Phyllida, a name I've never heard before or since. She was lumpy-looking and reminded me of a small loaf of bread baked in an oven with uneven heating. She wore a dress with tiny yellow flowers on it and pince-nez glasses on her nose. She and two men had the task of examining, then talking about, a multifaceted glass bottle at great length before they all guessed what the price was. The closest guesser got to take the bottle home. It was so painful and slow, it was as if "The Price Is Right" had gone into labor. Before the discussion even started, the glass bottle slowly revolved on a plinth while for ten minutes an elderly male commentator in a monotone voice described its history and each of its measurements.

55

EATING OUT AND OTHER RISKS

m y parents often said that everything in England tended to extremes. They were either very good or very bad. Because Mom and Dad had early experiences of rotten English food, they quickly purchased *The Good Food Guide*. This book, desperately needed by diners to avoid indigestion or worse, sold briskly. If you wanted good food in those days you had to know where to look. One could eat top-notch tea cakes at Claridge's, or at the other end of the spectrum, consume sandwiches filled with Marmite or Bovril, a dark brown yeasty spread with the taste of salt and the texture of petroleum jelly, at a local tea shop with sticky tables and spotty floors.

The Good Food Guide played the role of our family Bible. It was always visible and my parents consulted it constantly. Sensing its importance, I read it often, understanding about half of it at most, but realizing its worth to my family. The Bible is supposed to save people, but *The Good Food Guide* saved us—from ruined evenings and stomach cramps. While some children memorize Bible verses, I memorized pieces of *The Good Food Guide* without even trying because I read it so often. I learned that the best wine was "chateau-bottled" although I still haven't a clue what that means.

The author, an eccentric tycoon named Raymond Postgate, urged his readers to taste food "with a pure palate. Before tasting, clean it with bread and salt." Postgate railed about the "sins of innkeepers," chastising them for "the overall absence of fresh vegetables." He reminded his readers not to smoke over glasses of wine, as this was "a sign that the wine is too poor to trouble about" but that "this insult may of course be deserved." Some of his advice was so odd that I later wondered if he had early-onset Alzheimers. As the 1968 edition was his last, perhaps so.

He did us one enormous favor. Under the book's tutelage we found The Good Friends Chinese restaurant in the East End, which won a Good Food Award, whose recipients were decided at the whim of Postgate himself. The Good Friends was run by a Chinese immigrant named Charlie Cheung. Mr. Cheung lived and worked in the East End because he was forced to live there. Great prejudice against the Chinese and most foreigners existed in England in the 1950s (not that it's completely gone today). But we were the beneficiaries of his culinary skills when we crossed town to eat at his restaurant. Those were the most delicately crisp egg rolls and succulent sweet and sour prawns I've ever tasted.

Because of the "Law of British Extremes" previously mentioned, it held true that the restaurant immediately next to the Good Friends, named Lou's Fish and Chips, was horrible. We walked past Lou's to get to The Good Friends, and inevitably there would be a half-consumed bottle of orange drink in the window. The potato fryer would have grease, crumbs, and chip fragments all over it. Lisa and I were allowed to wander around outside while our parents had their post-meal conversation. We loved walking past Lou's front window with its greasy chip fryer and overall filth, pointing with ghoulish delight and saying, "Eeeeew!"

We also came upon a creepy, ivy-covered, deteriorating stone church surrounded by a cemetery with gray mossy stones. The thick canopy of trees above made the church and the tombstones of its honored dead very dark. We called it the "Haunted Graveyard" and spent many creepy, happy times there making ghost-noises, which we learned from watching Scooby-Doo, which was of course not on BBC 2.

We had a restaurant experience that was traumatic for my mother. We often patronized Murano's family restaurant in Kensington High Street.

We went there so often in 1969 that we developed a relationship with the kindly Mr. and Mrs. Murano. Then came the day we were eating lunch at a slightly wobbly table that faced the flight of stairs leading down to the kitchen below. My two-year-old brother Hankley had a sudden leg twitch, and kicked over the table. All the dishes, glasses, and condiments crashed to the floor, then rolled down the steps, cracking, shattering, and making tinkling noises all the way. The crashing and rolling and *tinkle-tinkle-tinkle* seemed to go on for a full five minutes. Mom was horrified and immediately offered to pay. The good owners refused. "Ah, he's just a child," they said with pained smiles. A month later, they went out of business. I don't know whether we caused it, but Mom never got over the guilt.

Mom knew that events could take a turn for the worse when the situation involved kids, dogs, and restaurants. We used to go eat at the British European Airways (BEA) Air Terminal, just down the street from Heathrow Airport, when BEA was still an airline. They had surprisingly good food there and, as in some European restaurants, dogs were allowed. Lisa at that time had Charles, her Cavalier Spaniel, so she entered the restaurant with the animal on a leash, looking forward to her upcoming cheeseburger. Just as we got in the door, but before anyone greeted us, Charles performed a fecal explosion. Mom commanded Lisa to disappear with the guilty dog before the staff could see who was responsible, but a crowd of diners lost their appetite that day.

56

HANKLEY GETS OLDER

I was convinced that my brother Hankley would stay a baby forever, but to my surprise, he got bigger, transformed into a child, and became interesting. Once he could talk, we became friends after a fashion. Hankley, as the youngest sibling, always wanted to tag along with his older sisters if he could. He always had his own priorities, however, and marched to the beat of his own drummer. He knew he would become an engineer in the way some children know from their earliest days that they will be doctors.

We saw this clearly the day we took a trip to the Regent's Park Zoo in London. We arrived at the front gate of this famous, giant zoo excited about viewing all the animals. Off to the side, there was a road repair crew. And then…Hankley spotted the Cement Mixer. It deserves to be capitalized, for Hankley was captivated by it. He told us that he wanted to stay and watch it go around. And around. And around. Then he wanted to talk to the operator about the mechanics involved with making a cement mixer revolve. Mom took Lisa and me inside for a happy afternoon observing tawny lions, giant grey hippos, and majestic tigers. Dad and Hankley spent the entire time observing the cement mixer creating concrete, contemplating the hand-held jackhammer and the air compressor that powered it as it blasted through the road. Dad and Hankley also got into a long conversation with the construction crew foreman about the composition of asphalt crack sealants. Hankley was ecstatic. Dad drank more than his usual quantity of wine that night and made a few references to a headache.

Hankley got his wishes fulfilled and his engineering dreams magnified that day. He did find out that his ambition had limits, though. A few years later, our family spent a few days in Pittsburgh on our way back to England. We went up the Duquesne Incline. It was a cable line that ran up the mountain. An old lantern swung from the ceiling of the century-old cable car. It was exciting to get to the top and look at downtown Pittsburgh far below from the observation deck. After we got off, my mother and sister and I enjoyed the view. My brother had eyes only for the machinery.

He gazed with rapt attention through the glass at all the gears and pulleys that moved the cable car up the incline. Clearly the four-year-old engineer inside him was on full alert. He turned to my mother and asked, "Can you give me that for Christmas?"

He was always tuned in to the physical realities of the world. The future engineer at age five studied cherry gelatin with fruit cocktail in it and announced to his family that he liked eating "crowded Jell-O." The way the pieces of fruit cocktail hung in space in the gelatin, seemingly defying the law of gravity, fascinated him. When beef stew was on the menu, he gently put his spoon into it and swirled it around.

"What are you doing stirring that stew around?" Mom asked him.

Hankley skimmed his spoon across the top of the steaming bowl. "Beef stew is the only thing we eat that has bubbles that stretch."

I hoped someday we would return to Pittsburgh. In addition to the Duquesne Incline, we got to stay in the penthouse suite at the Pittsburgh Hilton since we were on Dad's company tab. Room service was a delicious discovery. The idea that a person could pick up the phone and order anything he or she desired, then witness the appearance of someone carrying that very item on a tray, seemed like magic. Of course, I wasn't the one paying the bill at the time.

My friends have observed that to this day I love to stay in hotels. It isn't that the hotels are always great, but the memories certainly are.

57

ENTRY INTO SOUTH AMERICA

After we got back from living in Sao Paulo, people that my kinfolks knew in the Midwest would say, "You lived in Brazil? You mean Brazil, Indiana?" When I told them no, it was Brazil, South America, their faces would twist into an expression of bewildered disbelief at the idea of living in what was to them a wild, untamed place.

Our Uncle Gilbert, the same uncle who bought sheep with Uncle Ronald and later told Uncle Ronald that his share of the sheep died, invested in some Spotted Asses. They were really called that. It was some kind of cross-bred donkey. He took his Spotted Asses to a Spotted Ass Show in a town near Normalville. Our family, along with many of our extended family, attended. We won a door prize for coming the farthest distance. The announcer boomed over the PA system, "We have the Locasio family here, folks! They came all the way from Brazil, South America, to attend this Spotted Ass show, folks! Isn't that something, folks!"

Small towns have a charming way of framing events so that everything revolves around their town. In later years, when I worked at a church in Medina, Texas, population about 500, I saw the same phenomenon. At that time, the town hosted the Annual Medina International Apple Festival, complete with a Miss Apple Dumpling contest (for small girls) and a Miss Apple Blossom contest (for mature women), and Tri-Apple-On races. At a planning committee meeting after the first festival to plan the second festival, Judge Hatfield, who was chairing the committee, said that Miss Thelma had taken her festival tote bag along on her recent vacation in Paris. "They even know about us in Europe!" the man exclaimed.

We moved to Sao Paulo in 1973 after Dad's consulting project ended with the British Steel Corporation. By that time, European steel companies were ready to use their own people and not hire expensive American consultants anymore. The future lay in developing countries. I vividly remember our first night there. Charles, Lisa's Cavalier Spaniel, went with us, of course. He flew in cargo. The flight we took from Paris to Rio de Janeiro was long—it took us 13 hours non-stop. After that, we had to take another flight to Sao Paulo's Virocopas Airport.

When we finally arrived, we checked in at the Sao Paulo Hilton where we would be staying for a month until our house was ready. Exhausted and culture-shocked, three children with Charles, piled into room 1206 while my parents were next door in 1205. We had a door adjoining the two rooms that Mom unlocked so she could check on us. My parents ordered dinner for us in 1206 via room service. Fortunately, as they catered to international travelers from all over the world, they spoke good English. Just before our food arrived, Charles pulled a similar stunt to the one he had performed at the BEA Air Terminal in London three years before. No doubt traumatized by the long plane trip in a crate, he moved his bowels substantially.

Then the waiter knocked on the door with our cart. Crisis! Dogs were barely tolerated at this hotel and this could have sent us packing. "Quick! Run next door!" my fast-thinking mother commanded. We all rushed into 1205 and locked the adjoining door, concealing the horror in the next room. My father opened the door to 1205 with his most genial smile. "Sorry, *senor*! We're over here!" That was the one time I was thankful my father was such a good liar.

The Hilton swimming pool was on the top floor. It was possible to see over the wall to the traffic 30 stories below. We met an American boy named Billy at the pool one day. His father, like ours, was an American consultant. Billy was staying at the hotel at company expense with his mother while they looked for housing. Billy pointed out that in addition to seeing over the wall, we could launch a paper airplane over it. We did.

We whooped and clapped as the airplane swirled, looped in circles, got caught by the wind, and spiraled down in a gentle descent that took a full five minutes, at least in my recollection, as I'm not a Physics major. At last, the plane made its descent to traffic level. It landed on someone's windshield. Even all those levels up, we heard a piercing squeal of brakes and saw cars swerve, barely missing each other. We did not tell our parents about this adventure.

Our six months in Brazil were an exercise in learning not to take for granted some services that were basic in places we had previously lived. Our phone worked about half the time. There were no current maps of the city because construction was proceeding so fast, it was out of sync with the map makers. We lived in Sao Paulo because that's where the company's headquarters were located, but Dad did most of his work in Belo Horizonte, which had an infrastructure even more primitive than Sao Paulo's. While he worked there, we communicated over a shortwave radio, with my father's voice's volume rising and falling amidst the static in the background.

I wish we could have transplanted the house we lived in, though. It was located at the corner of *Rua Caiubi* and *Joaquim Nabuco*, a busy inter-section near both the Jumbo (Joom-Boh) Supermarket and a massive *favela* (shanty town) area full of metal shacks, its orange and yellow façade rose gracefully to dominate the street. The house had a huge dining room with shining light wood floors, a living room, six bedrooms, five bathrooms, and a party room with a men's and women's restroom in it. The men's restroom had a urinal. Lisa and I would tease Hankley by saying we were going to use the boys' bathroom and pee in the urinal. Hankley would get massively upset. "You're going in the BOYS TOILET! But you're a GIRL!" By the age of five, Hankley was well aware of gender roles and differences.

We rode our bikes around in the party room. It was big enough for that. It also had a built-in barbecue pit with a chimney. Near the barbecue pit there was a dumb waiter, a miniature elevator that ascended to the kitchen and came back down to us with the touch of a button. A kitchen maid could put drinks in it and send them down to the party. We used to put the dog in it and ride him up and down. No wonder Charlie became neurotic in his old age. Long before the show *Lifestyles of the Rich and Famous* came along, we lived it, if only for a short while.

We had three servants, Francisco the chauffeur, Irene (pronounced *ee-ray-nee*) his wife who was the maid, and Yvonne (*ee-voh-nee*) the cook. Francisco and Irene did not get along at all with Yvonne. We heard screaming matches in Portuguese in the servants' quarters at times. My mother, who did not understand the language, was at a loss to know what the continuous melodrama was about. Finally, she asked a bilingual Brazilian, the woman next door, to help her. The woman went down to visit the three warring servants and listened a while. Then she came upstairs and told my mother, "Francisco and Irene like to eat black beans. Yvonne insists on cooking red ones."

The servants ate *arroz e feijao* (rice and beans) as a staple. I sometimes joined them. I found that I liked the taste of the two together. My mother, ever the aristocrat, was not happy about it. Rich Americans didn't eat rice and beans. Now I know they're nutritious and, especially if it's brown rice, it makes a complete meal. When we went to the Jumbo grocery store, there were three or four enormous aisles full of nothing but pasta in every shape and beans of every color. Those were the foods on which the vast majority of Brazilians subsisted. As in Germany, the grocery store revealed much about the culture.

Francisco was as stupid as a pile of those beans. He made the same joke over and over. He would address Charlie, saying *"Bem cachorro!"* (Good dog!) Then he would solemnly tell Charlie, "Francisco *nao falo-ingles!* Francisco *Portugues!"* As if Charlie's inability to communicate vocally with Francisco was due to a language barrier. The first time Francisco did this I laughed. By the time he had done it every day for a month, it became a bit tiring.

The faces of the *favela* children still haunt me. When we swam in our outdoor pool, these little ones would gather quietly at the gate to watch us. Their faces had no anger, blame, or judgment on them. They just looked hungry and sad. My parents insisted that we not feed them. "If you feed one, a mob of them will swarm you," my father warned. If one of them asks you for food, say, *"Nao tem!"* Which meant, I don't have it. Dad did not seem to mind or notice the children. My mother did. She said they bothered her, whether because their poverty was uncomfortable or whether she felt genuinely sorry for them I don't know.

I came to understand why rich people live behind high fences and locked gates, though.

58

CATHOLIC SCHOOL SURPRISES

Guilt tripper: Brazilian is coffee good...and expensive. Too bad the water in Brazil tastes so bad—a bitter metallic taste. The locals may never know how good their coffee tastes.

attended *Escola Maria Immaculada*, or the School of Mary Immaculate, the American Catholic School. I wanted to attend Graded, the American secular school, but my father had heard it had a drug problem. He also said the lockers were bent at the corners from students trying to break in and steal the contents. No hall passes were required, and it was possible to cut classes as oversight was lax. "The Catholics at least exercise some discipline," he told us. I thought that the Graded school sounded like more fun, but Dad was adamant.

The school was unlike any I had attended before. Due to the warm weather, the hallways were not enclosed. When we went from one classroom to another, we had a roof overhead, but we walked outdoors. It was a novelty being instructed by nuns in full white habits and giant silver crosses around their necks. I learned to say the Hail Mary and the Catholic version of the "Lord's Prayer" while wearing a white blouse and a blue plaid skirt. We all crossed ourselves each morning under the brusque but kindly leadership of Sister Mary Michaelette from Buffalo, New York. She had a voice with the volume set at foghorn, and was prone to say after praying, "Get your carcasses into your seats!"

Sister Michaelette took no nonsense from anyone. She was about forty-five years old, wore brown framed glasses and transported a stocky build under her white habit. She had a black belt in judo. Knowing that gave me the understanding that nuns are interesting people.

One day, a boy named George stood at attention, as required, but didn't cross himself or say the Hail Mary. Sister Michaelette demanded, "Why didn't you make the sign of the cross?"

"I'm not Catholic," George replied.

"In my classroom, you cross yourself like any good Catholic," Sister Michaelette rejoined, and made George say the Hail Mary all by himself.

One day, she announced to us that from now on, we were not to be in the hallways without a written pass. Tim Hansen, who sat diagonally in front of me, asked, "But what if I don't have time to get a pass? What if I have to go and throw up?"

Sister Michaelette rolled her eyes. "I'll follow you…with a pass."

The American eighth graders were academically behind me, but socially much more sophisticated from being at a co-ed school instead of a single-sex institution like the one I had attended in Europe. It was a stunning revelation to walk into that classroom the first day and see all the girls wearing skillfully applied makeup. That would never have been allowed at Godolphin and Latymer; there, makeup was strictly prohibited. One girl in particular, Julie, wore it lavishly and seemed to have false eyelashes, too.

After lunch one afternoon, red-haired Margaret was talking to her best friend, the popular brown-haired, blue-eyed Marianne. "You have to remember that even though Julie's done it and isn't innocent any more, she's not a whore and she's not a sexpot. She's a nice kid."

Marianne agreed that she and Margaret should tell everyone to be nice to Julie even through her misadventures with lovemaking. I'm not sure if Margaret was showing off her sophistication, trying to freak us out, or genuinely trying to protect Julie's reputation, but it caused me culture shock. This frank talk about sex and losing one's virginity was not remotely like the reserved English way of life I had known.

The boys made fun of my English accent, too. Junior high simply isn't a time when a person wants to stand out in any way. Phil Cooper, who sat at the back of the room, would wait for me to speak in class and then say in a perfect London accent, "Jolly good job!" Other boys would ask if I wanted a "spot of tea." I worked hard to rid myself of this hated way of speaking so I would fit in better and not be different. Not all of the teenagers teased me, however. Many showed friendly curiosity. Ana Kristina Metcalfe, who wore faint blue eye shadow and had a freckly pixie nose, was fascinated, and kind about it. "Tell me about London," she would encourage me.

I was socially isolated in the midst of these students. I experienced my first full-blown depression. Although I did not know the term "depression," the feeling was very real . I struggled against tears all the time. I went off alone during lunch at first, but Sister Michaelette did not allow it to continue. She asked Debbie Seawalk, Anna Viachek, and Madeline Bonilla to take me under their wing. They did, and they were wonderful. It was particularly good of Madeline, as she was one of the junior varsity cheerleaders and risked her social standing by reaching out to me.

Madeline was from Spain. She was pretty, easy-going, and good-natured. She would call out to her friends to get their attention by saying, "Hey! You with the head!" When five people would turn to stare, Madeline would crack up and so would they. I craved the kind of self-confidence with peers that Madeline had established.

Debbie, with her butt-length blond hair, gave me solemn lessons in the only things boys ever thought about, which, according to her, were sex and sports. She told me that I must never mention anything about sex, but she did teach me how to flirt, as I was clueless about such things. Debbie also told me never to say that I liked Donny Osmond. "Boys hate that," she advised, and she was right. She told me that other girls liked him, but the only appropriate place to exchange Donny Osmond or David Cassidy posters was in the girls' bathroom where boys would not see us. What the boys thought of us, I learned, was of the utmost importance.

The most discussed topic among those girls was always what boys were thinking. I was once careless and was seen holding the teen idol magazine *Tiger Beat*. I heard a couple of guys snorting behind me and saying, "those Osmond fags."

How I felt about myself was so tied to boys' good opinion of me or lack thereof. The desire for their approval had begun several years earlier when my cousin Mark crowned me Miss Beautiful Toiletwater. However, it became even more crucial to me as I got older. One night, when the pixie-like, snub-nosed, and boy-crazy Julie Stevens had us over for a party, she told Lisa, "You're so cute! And so funny! You're going to wind up with the sweetest and the cutest guy ever!" Then she looked at me and quickly looked away.

The following year, Mom and I were talking about boys. I was going into ninth grade, Lisa into eighth. Mom said, "Lisa will be more popular with boys than you. She's really funny, she's friendly, and she has a glow about her that you just don't have." Early in the school year, I had the chance to talk to a boy I liked in my English class, but I remembered what my mother said and did not reach out.

Not only were the American youth at the Catholic school sophisticated, they were also bilingual. Most of them had been at the school since kindergarten. Brazilian law required that every student be schooled in the native Portuguese, and my eighth-grade class knew enough of it to flip back and forth from English to Portuguese easily with each other. I remember a phrase of English being followed by a longer Portuguese sentence, followed by peals of laughter. We spoke English except in Portuguese class, but I only ever understood about half of the conversations anyone had outside of the classrooms.

One unusual event at the school that we actually enjoyed was when the assistant principal Sister Joan-Marie visited. This short, squat, elderly nun had square-framed black glasses, a massive under bite, and tiny sharp teeth. She got feverishly worked up over matters of discipline. When she visited our classroom, I always watched Sister Michaelette's body language. Sister Michaelette would sigh, pout, push out her lower lip, and visibly roll her eyes. Sister Joan-Marie would gesture wildly and yell about how students were "dropping f-f-f-food on the f-f-f-floor of the caf-f-f-eteria!" When she got going she not only stuttered, she spat. "When I was in school, we knew that FOOD was a GIFT from GOD!" she would exhort, pounding her fists into the air. "So when we dropped it, we had to P-P-PICK it off the F-F-FLOOR (flecks of drool would fly here) and KISS IT!" At least we had five minutes free from lessons to hear this.

I did not get along at all well with Astrid Hernandez, the girl with long dark hair, a sizable nose, and thick lips, who sat at the desk in the front row on my right. Astrid was from Chile and had been sent to Brazil to be educated at the school. She seemed to despise me from the first day I arrived. When I spilled paint in art class, she laughed and refused to help me clean it up. But these days, I feel a sense of poignancy about Astrid. I was at the school from January to June 1973. In September of 1973, her country experienced a coup in which the democratically elected leader, Salvador Allende, was assassinated, with the notorious Augusto Pinochet installed in his place. I hope Astrid survived through the coup and the Pinochet regime that followed, and went on to live a happy life.

A result from living in so many countries is that I now follow international news with more interest than many Americans. I know people in a lot of those places.

59

A MOST UNUSUAL PARTY...AND A SNAKE FARM

The cultural diversity of the school presented some unusual situations. In March, before winter's cold weather set in (need I say that Brazil's seasons are the reverse of the United States?) we were invited to Fernando Fonseca's party. Fernando's parents were wealthy. The Fonsecas lived in *Chacara Flora*, the most luxurious neighborhood of mansions in Sao Paulo. We arrived late, my father having dropped us off in our opulent Ford Galaxie. We were admitted by a maid who showed us to the back of the house where all the seventh- and eighth-graders were already celebrating. We were awed by the majestic white house and especially by the giant swimming pool, bathhouse, and lush lawn in the back. The pool glowed softly with green and blue underwater lighting.

To my surprise, my classmate Burke Hyde offered me a beer, which was freely available along with sweet wine. Fernando also passed around cigarettes. Within an hour, most of the kids were drunk. Marita, Astrid's best friend, had wandered into the bathhouse and found some shampoo. In her intoxicated state, she washed her hair in the pool and soon there were mounds of soap bubbles all over the surface.

When my father came to pick us up he saw all of the raucous teenagers. "I'm drunk as shit," a boy announced to him. "Absolutely stinko." He said it as if he had accomplished something admirable. The Fonseca party was a topic of shocked discussion among our parents for months.

☙

After school was out for the summer, the family took a day trip to the district of Butanta, near the campus of the University of Sao Paulo. The institute at Butanta these days is world-renowned for its collection of poisonous snakes, including its 407 varieties of cobra, as well as lizards, spiders, and other unpleasant creatures. If you go to their website, you'll see pictures of the snakes hanging out in an area surrounded by high fences. When we went there 40 years ago, we peered over the snake pits, which were not protected by anything. My mother gripped my small brother as he leaned over and her knuckles turned white. There were curled-up cobras sleeping, their coils piled up high.

Inside, there were glass cases of tarantulas. I tapped the glass and woke up a sleeping arachnid, which waggled a hairy leg at me, whether in friendliness or anger I don't know and don't care. At least none of us fell in a snake pit that day.

The Butanta Snake Institute is a leading producer of vaccines and curative serum. According to its website, it leads scientific missions at home and abroad through the World Organization and Pan American Health Organization, UNICEF and the UN, and cooperates in fighting epidemics of disease. Blessings on them. That's good work, but better them than me.

We got lost returning from Butanta. We had taken this trip without our new chauffeur, Alfredo Nundez, who had a great sense of direction and could find anything. My father could not. We got stuck in a loop, going around and around a giant block of twisting roadway and coming again and again to the same intersection. In desperation, my father took a new turn just to try something different. Suddenly, we heard a loud rattling and bumping sound. We had driven over a large, twisted piece of barbed wire in the road and it had decimated one of our back tires.

It was getting dark. We were all nervous. We were in a residential district, but not one with which we were familiar. Dad went to get the jack and the spare tire out of the trunk. He had not changed a tire in years, but he assured us that he remembered how. And then the miracle happened. Out of the darkness a voice called out. "Hey! Are you all right?" It was a man's voice. In this Portuguese-speaking country, it called to us in English. My father shouted back, saying we had a flat. A blond young man came out of the house near where our tire had been destroyed.

"Your family can come inside," he urged. "I'll help you with the tire. My wife will get you some lemonade." They were a Swedish family. We visited with the woman and her two long-haired daughters while Dad and the nameless Swede changed the tire. After we finished the refreshments, he gave my father directions home. Perhaps there really are guardian angels out there; what are the odds that we would gash our tire in the middle of a residential neighborhood in a foreign country and the first voice we would hear calling out to us spoke English?

The rest of my Brazilian memories consist of trivia. The next door neighbor girl, a sixth-grader called Lucille Bishop who was half English and half Brazilian, taught us to curse in Brazilian Portuguese. She said that the Portuguese word for "fucked" was *"fudeu,"* but that this word was not as vulgar as it was in English. *"Merde"* was a shitty word, literally, and one did not say it in polite company. According to Lucille, the most disgusting word of all in Portuguese was *"puta"* which means prostitute. To call a man a *"filho da puta"* was to invite a fist in one's face.

I wonder if all young foreign language learners acquire the swear words first. They are almost the only Portuguese words I remember. Obviously they meant a lot to me.

As I may be the only person around who can swear in Brazilian Portuguese as it was spoken in 1973, if anyone needs this essential skill I will send them a resume. They could have called me at my Brazilian home phone number, 616 313, or *Seis Um Seis, Tres Um Tres.* That also stuck with me for some reason. If you had wanted to call me in London in the late 1960s the number was 229-0860. Later, as a teenager, you would have had to call 238-5951. Useless information now, but like the song "Let It Go" from the movie *Frozen,* it has stuck firmly in my head. I can't seem to let any of it go.

The rest of learning Portuguese ranged from futile to painful. Our young female Portuguese teacher at Escola Maria Imaculada had short red hair, brown eyes, and a perpetual worried look on her face. She could not keep order in the classroom. We would periodically stop work when Kenneth Free, a seventh-grade star basketball player and class clown combined, would start singing, "Oh I wish I was an Oscar Meyer Weiner! That is what I truly want to be-ee-ee! And if I was an Oscar Meyer Weiner, everyone would be in love with ME!" At the end of the song he would add, "But everyone's in love with me already, so who cares!"

Poor *Senorita* Teacher. I forget her name. It was as unimportant as anything she taught. The class only calmed down when Sister Joan Marie came storming in. "Stop it!" she would yell, spitting drool as always. "Be quiet, and write down fifty nouns, fifty verbs, and fifty adjectives in Portuguese!"

We would say, "But Sister, we don't know that many!"

"Well! Write ten then!" The sister would stomp off and we would write down a few words while Kenneth softly resumed, "I wish I was an Oscar Meyer Weeeeeiner..."

That was the futile part of Portuguese. The painful part of it was playing *queimada*, the Portuguese word for dodgeball. It was all we ever did in gym class. Marilou, our beefy dark-skinned Portuguese-speaking gym teacher was nicknamed, "Dynamite Lou" for reasons I never understood. She seemed to know no other activities for a gym class besides playing *queimada*. So I got to relive bittersweet summer evenings with Cousin Mark, but in a class of socially sophisticated girls who, like Mark, had all the athletic ability I lacked. The one silver lining in the cloud was that they were so invested in being feminine that they didn't throw a ball as hard as Mark did. My strategy was to be hit with the ball early to get it over with, and then go sit in the corner and stare into space while the others finished the game.

I learned to fake allergies to cover up the tears in the girls' locker room after gym period. Are physical education classes, showers, and locker rooms recalled as torture chambers in anyone else's memory?

In addition to being a disaster at *queimada*, I worried constantly about my breast size. Too large or too small?

In the locker room, when my bilingual peers switched over from English to say, "*Que é para o almoço hoje?* meaning "What's for lunch today?" It was all too easy to imagine they were asking why my breast size was so far beyond normal. The experience of being so often, and without warning, surrounded by people speaking a language I didn't understand has given me great compassion for foreigners and refugees living in America. There is nothing like having been there yourself to impart this kind of understanding.

60
THE EMERGING ENGINEER

We finally returned to the United States in time for me to start high school. Dad could see that the Sao Paulo gig wasn't working. Mom was starting to act weird. She began to say that she was afraid to eat Brazilian vegetables because they were fertilized with human shit. She got obsessed with my eating beans and rice. "You'll get fat. And sick," she worried. She hated to let Lisa or me leave the house without her. "There's safety in numbers," she pleaded. And she wasn't sleeping well. So Dad resigned his job with Booz Allen & Hamilton, took another position, and we ended up in Ohio where Mom took antidepressants for a while.

When I was well along in high school, three major things happened that I remember to this day. One, I got to see Hankley's emerging creativity. He designed mazes and board games and wrote a detective story. Two, the mishaps on our family car trips that we started taking when we returned to the United States. Three, my father's foray into Transcendental Meditation.

Hankley tried to get me to do the mazes he drew. It drove me nuts. He said, "Here's a huge maze. Look, it has a present inside for you." He had drawn a box in the center of the maze with a bow on it.

"Big deal," I growled.

Hankley went away, came back, and said, "Here's a better maze. It has a DIAMOND in the middle!" He was a great maze builder, but had trouble understanding how to set up an incentive plan.

He invented a board game similar to Monopoly. In addition to squares all around the outside of the board, he had paths that led to one space in the center. From that space a player was allowed to choose which direction to go. Hankley called that the "Square of Indecision." Another square carried a penalty for landing on it. Hankley wrote, "You must relinquish five hundred dollars." I suppose one could get away with not paying the money if they didn't understand what "relinquish" meant. We teased Hankley by saying that before attempting the game, players had to get a college degree.

We did enjoy it when his English teacher in the Gifted and Talented Program assigned him the project of writing a short story in the sixth grade. It had to be of some substantial length—a page or two would not suffice. Hankley was not happy about it. He liked math and science much better, but resigned himself to his fate. The result was his one and only detective masterpiece, which he called "The Wriley Children." The Wriley Children were a gang of five brothers and sisters, patterned on the Hardy Boys and Nancy Drew, who were crackerjack detectives with a bent for chasing down Russian spies. We knew that, because the children rode in the back seat of the car with their father to the airport and watched a plane disembark that had Russian spies on it. When they saw three swarthy men in dark glasses coming off the plane, Steve Wriley, the oldest, pointed at them and said, "Look! Russian spies!" So we knew it had to be true. It worked for the Hardy Boys and James Bond, anyway.

Mr. Wriley, their father, seems not to have shared the brilliance of his progeny. Hankley wrote about him coming home one night and calling to his wife. "Honey! I have good news!"

"Oh, that's wonderful, dear," answered Mrs. Wriley. "What's your news?"

Mr. Wriley announced, "After twenty-five years, I have finally found myself a job!"

Following this exchange, and with the Wriley children no doubt reassured by their father's new-found employment, the kids went to scope out the three Russian spies they had discovered earlier.

On their patrol, Steve Wriley, the leader of the gang, began by instructing his siblings, "Go and take a look around, and report back to me any suspicious buildings you may find."

At this point we were laughing too hard to continue. "Hey!" I gasped to my brother between giggles. "I just found a very suspicious skyscraper! I KNOW it wasn't there yesterday!"

61

CRUISING IN THE CAR

The second memory of late adolescence was of multiple family car trips. At last we were acting like real 1970s Americans, which meant buying two cars, guzzling lots of gas, and logging miles on the highway. When we were teenagers, one of the best parts of being back in the United States was that we could visit our grandparents in Indiana much more often. At Christmas, sometimes at spring break, and always for a couple of weeks or more in the summer, we took trips in the family car to see our relatives.

Most times, those excursions were uneventful, but not always. There was, for example, the trip when I almost strangled Hankley with my bare hands. He was sitting in the middle seat in the back of the car. "Ann, could you roll down your window? I have to throw my gum out." I rolled the window down and told him to be careful. Hankley removed the gum from his mouth and threw it hard into the wind. Next thing I knew, there was an explosion of laughter from Hankley, "Ann!" He giggled so hard he could hardly speak, "I think you'll have to wash your hair tonight."

I sat for the next three hours with Dubble Bubble dangling from my bangs and my brother intermittently exploding with mirth. The gum didn't come out in the shower; I had to cut it out and walk around with a chunk of hair missing until it grew back. It's amazing I let Hankley live to adulthood.

Sometimes, though, I was the one who blew it. One time on a summer family car trip, we stopped at a truck stop in the middle of nowhere near the Indiana border. This was long before the days of ubiquitous Dairy Queens and golden arches. The only option for miles would be Stuckey's, which we hated. They were old, dirty, run-down, and had stale food and foul-smelling restrooms. Their motto should have been "Stuckey's, Because You're Stuck with Us." But that day we were desperate for a rest stop and a drink of water so we pulled in the Stuckey's that was located at the next exit. There were many cars, presumably with other desperate motorists inside. There were even more big rigs parked in the vast parking lot. We went inside and ordered the usual hot dogs served in cardboard trays with cardboard buns. We were surrounded by truck drivers. To this day I blame my immature adolescent brain for what I said. I looked around me at the truckers and told my mother, sister, and brother in too loud a voice, "You know who looks like a trucker? Our neighbor Mr. Clovis! Because his teeth are falling out and they're all yellow!"

Mom's eyes widened like saucers. "SSSSSH!" she gasped.

Then a burly African-American trucker turned and looked at us. He said, "Well, I seen some office workers that ain't so good-lookin' either!" While I blushed the deepest hue of scarlet possible, the man came over to sit near us and told us how the Teamsters Union actually provided a fine dental plan to its truckers, giving the lie to my statement. He seemed to go on for a very long time, explaining the details of tooth care for truck drivers. When at last he finished and went back to the table with his friends, my sister laughed for what seemed like forever. It seemed that whenever we passed a truck stop from then on, Lisa would say, "I wonder if there are truckers in there that look like Mr. Clovis? You know, with teeth falling out? And all yellow!" I never heard the end of it.

Sometimes trips went wrong without anyone screwing up. The snafus just happened. We were traveling through open countryside one summer afternoon on the way to Indiana with cornfields endlessly skimming past our car windows. We were hungry and thirsty and ready for a drink of water and a refreshing ice cream. But as luck so often had it in those days, we were near no towns or recognizable brand-name restaurants.

To this day, I wonder why my mother did not plan for such exigencies by packing a cooler. But she was not fond of anything to do with picnics or camping. Blue-blooded aristocrat that she was, such activities were for poor people, and not something with which she wanted to involve herself.

But because of Mom's aversion to picnics and coolers, we repeatedly found ourselves miles from decent sized cities or passable places to eat. On this occasion, we finally saw a large green directional sign for a town called West Salem. We got off at the exit and drove a few miles to the town to find the ice cream parlor. We circled the commercial area and at last discovered the only place selling ice cream.

It was a dilapidated kiosk. A wooden sign hung crookedly from the roof on a rusty chain saying DAIREE-FREEZ. As we approached the window, we caught the sharp odor of sour milk. Mom wrinkled her nose. "Let's not do this," she snapped. She pivoted around and marched back to the car.

Frustrated and disappointed, we drove on for another few hours. Unpleasant as it was, this memorable incident took a place of honor in our family folklore. Never again did we set off on a family trip without someone piping up, "Remember, we have to allow lots of extra time! We have to stop at the West Salem Dairee-Freez!"

62

TRANSCENDENTAL MEDITATION

My father's business skill was accounting and presenting its results. He also used his toolbox well for household repairs. He was a thoroughly practical man who thought that most children "didn't make themselves useful enough." He and my mother were a good match partly for this reason. Neither one of them was a particularly imaginative parent, but they understood the importance of routine and structure in bringing up children. We had few forays into creativity with them; we provided that for ourselves. We did learn mundane skills. We learned to budget and save money, make to-do lists, join Triple A in case of car trouble, and when we had a social event, ensure there was plenty of toilet paper. These are not glamorous learnings, but they're important. I have been with fellow employees whose paychecks got held up for some reason, and they had to live on credit cards because they had no money saved. With the parents I had, that would not happen to me in a million years.

So it came as a surprise when my father took a sudden desire to explore Transcendental Meditation (TM) when I was a high school upperclassman. He was experiencing considerable stress at work, so possibly desperation drove him to it. Being the family man he was, he decided to seek a remedy for his stress that involved bringing the rest of us along with him. In those days, Transcendental Meditation was popular. The Beatles had brought it to our attention several years earlier by going to India and learning it from the Maharishi Mahesh Yogi. The newspapers were now running glowing reports on its benefits. By 1976, mainstream business executives, mostly men who could afford it, were starting to check it out.

One chilly night in the fall in our Cleveland suburb, my father came home from work and announced that he had made an appointment at a local Transcendental Meditation Center for himself, my mother, sister, brother, and me. By golly, we were all going to learn how to meditate. I was intrigued. My father was not even a churchgoer at that time. He scorned anything psychic or not of the material world. He spent weekends doing household repairs and yard work, reading the paper, smoking cigars, and watching sports. This announcement about TM seemed completely out of character.

But that dark rainy October night, he shepherded us into the gold family Oldsmobile Cutlass, to introduce us to TM. I remember little about the exterior of the TM center; it was probably a bland office building. However, entering it presented a rich visual display. As soon as we went through the door, we were greeted with portraits of Indian TM masters and landscapes of beautiful Asian countryside. There was a substantial color photo of the Taj Mahal.

In addition to the fee, my father was instructed over the phone in advance to bring several pieces of fruit, a bunch of flowers, and a handkerchief for each family member. Upon arrival and sign-in, and after my father had a hefty chunk of cash extracted from his MasterCard, each of us was escorted separately to meet with our personal TM teacher. Mine was a man of around thirty-five, with sandy blond hair and glasses. His slightly glazed eyes suggested he might have smoked substantial weed in the previous decade.

However, he was a brilliant performer. I handed over to him my bag containing fruit, flowers, and handkerchief. Then he explained to me that before we got to the business of learning TM, I would witness a ceremony of tribute to the grand master Maharishi Mahesh Yogi. There was an altar in the room covered with a white cloth, upon which stood a crystal vase, a bronze dish, and two white scented candles on either side. Above the altar hung a portrait of the Maharishi, smiling benignly in his white robe, long dark hair and mustache, dark brown eyes, and white beard.

The Teacher, who had impressed me enough to think of his title in capital letters, lit the candles and put the flowers in the vase. He piled the fruit into the bronze dish. As he covered the fruit with the handkerchief, he gazed at the portrait of the Maharishi and began to chant in what was presumably Sanskrit. At age sixteen, I had never seen anything like it. "Maharishi Yuma Sang Ra Hari Krishna Hallelujah Hall of Famer," I heard, or something similar. It seemed genuine given the Teacher's intensity, but who knows?

After witnessing the ceremony, I would have believed anything the Teacher said. He then explained to me the benefits of practicing TM, which included my grades going up in school. As I was enrolled in a difficult chemistry class, that got my attention. Continued practice of meditation meant a more relaxed attitude at all times, an abundance of joy, and eventually "cosmic consciousness," when one attained that blissful state.

The Teacher stressed that when one attained that blissful state, they might be stabbed with a knife, but would feel no fear.

It would hurt, but I would feel no fear.

I was sure it was true. He then went on to give me my mantra, a Sanskrit word that I must never reveal to anyone, ever. That word was "*Eye-Ing*." I still wonder if that word was unique to me or if everyone got the same word. Or if there was a list of fifty cool words that got distributed in order and then they started over.

The effect of all this was several months of meditation and not much else before we gradually gave it up. One evening on his way home from work on the bus, my father fell asleep while meditating and slobbered all over his tie. He wondered when he got home, "What do they do with guys who slop their mantras?"

My mother practiced it longer than anyone else because my mother is the type who will persist long after others give up. I still got the C in chemistry that I feared, but it has not ruined my life.

In retrospect, my father seemed to genuinely want to find a way for all of us to handle stress. Too bad we couldn't have attended a Buddhist temple and gotten all of this for free. Those Sanskrit mantras must have been the most expensive words on record. But money isn't everything. The TM encounter sparked my lifelong love affair with the spiritual, mysterious, and otherworldly.

I wonder if my accountant father thought it was worth it when the MasterCard bill arrived?

Last

REVELATIONS, BACKSTORIES, AND MOVING ON

Living in the United States was plain vanilla compared to the fiesta of flavorful living in Wales, Germany, England, and Brazil. I didn't like every single flavor there, or every custom, language, or habit we practiced. But it was never dull. Returning to American soil, I passed the usual milestones of Driver's Ed, getting a license, fulfilling my high school class requirements, and graduating. My patchwork childhood prepared me for a highly complex young adulthood to come.

My mother passed away a year ago. After she got Parkinson's disease, Hankley and his wife moved her to a board and care home. They went through her old letters. She had sent a pile of them, over time, to her mother in Normalville when our family lived overseas. She pleaded for Grandma Miller to pray for the family. In her elegant script handwriting amidst many deletions and crossings-out, my mother had inscribed a family secret which she never talked about. She wrote this.

"Dear Mother,

I hope you and everyone in Normalville are fine. Please pray for Vic and me and the girls. As I write, Vic is curled up on the living room sofa, refusing to go to work. He's got the depression real bad. His boss calls every day, threatening to come over. If he comes over and sees Vic, he'll fire him. I'm frightened that we'll end up on welfare. I don't think I can support the girls on a music teacher's salary. I'm so worried! Yesterday when Mr. Rhodes called, I told him that Vic had a physical complaint. I said we'd been to the city hospital, and they'd know real soon what was wrong with him. I don't want to lie to the boss, but I don't know what else to do. Please pray for us.

Love,
Betty

I do not know how she kept the boss at bay, but she did. She may have done it many times. I will always wonder how she pulled it off. What combination of anger, pleading, and persuasion did she use to get my father off the couch and back to work? I wish I could ask her. It is wonderful what we can do when we have to.

My father kept his job and most every job thereafter until I left home. Financially we always did fine. I wondered often as a child why my mother was always worrying out loud, "We're going to run out of money!" I wondered why she felt so constantly threatened. I was perplexed that her life with us children brought her so little joy. Now I know that whether or not we had to get on public assistance depended on whether my mother could get my father to go to work. My mother often said, "We've got one foot in the grave, and the other on a banana peel." Now I understand why.

For all the mean things Mom said to me, she fought tooth and nail to keep the family together. We had food on the table, clothes on our backs, and a great education. What a fighter. Mom was tough and brave. She did the best she could. And now, as a woman in my fifties with twinkly eyes behind my glasses and all the gray hairs I've earned, I honor that. My mother and I both graduated from the School of Hard Knocks. If we have nothing else in common, at least there's that.

A week ago, riding to work, I had a vision. I boarded the Austin Cap Metro 300 bus and prepared to face my employment challenges that day. Standing and blocking my favorite seat stood an African-American man. He could have sat there and I wouldn't have minded, but why did he have to block me from doing so? That seat was, and is, my favorite place to distract myself by observing the world outside the bus. I sat down in my fourth or fifth favorite seat and started to ruminate about karma catching up with that man someday. My irritation must have showed on my face, because he said, "If it bothers you, ma'am, I'll sit down. It's just that I'm tired. If I sit down I might fall asleep and miss my stop."

I took a closer look at this man who had just told me, "It wasn't about you." He looked exhausted. His face was lined and his eyes drooped. Probably he was homeless or working two jobs. I realized that none of what he was doing had anything to do with me. Then the vision began.

The worst coworker I ever had showed up and said, "It wasn't about you. I didn't mean to be bossy and impossible to work with. I was busting my butt to get a desperately-needed promotion."

My sister appeared, 22 years after committing suicide. "It wasn't about you," she said. "I treated you mean because I thought you were stealing Mom and Dad's love from me. Every time you did more, I felt myself being loved less. Do you understand how scared I was?"

My father put in an appearance next. "It wasn't about you," he explained. "You weren't the reason I drank. It was the bad memories. My father beat me with a belt. I was abused by a Catholic priest at the age of five. I was threatened with hellfire and damnation at my grandmother's Pentecostal church. Then there was what happened when I was in World War II. I tried so hard to be a good Dad."

Finally, my mother appeared. "It wasn't about you, darlings," she said, putting her arm around my sister and reaching toward me. "I did what I knew how to do, which wasn't a lot. And by the time I made sure your father showed up to work and didn't drink himself to death, there wasn't much left to give."

"It wasn't about you…it wasn't about you…it wasn't about you…" All of them were saying the same thing. They smiled, while their eyes asked me the question, "Do you understand now?"

I turned to the tired man standing on the bus. "Come here, sir," I invited. "Have a seat. Rest your feet. Let's talk, and I'll make sure you don't fall asleep."

Acknowledgements

I owe a debt of gratitude to my two best friends. Kay Pruett has been with me through the agony and joy of writing and much else. She's a constant and caring presence as well as being a national Teacher of the Year for visually impaired youth. Also Donna Murphree, counselor extraordinaire, who is always ready to provide a shoulder to lean on, a laugh to count on, and countless games of cribbage. David and Nancy Mossman are part of my treasured inner circle as well. When things get stormy, they are a sure and steady refuge and we've enjoyed Thanksgivings, Christmases, and birthday celebrations together. All of these people are my "framily." Grateful thanks to my cousin Carol who supplied material for me. Also a tip of the hat to the good-natured staff of Quack's Bakery and Cafe where I wrote most of this book. For me it's the best coffee shop in Austin. And, I have to thank my late mother and father for having me, without which this book would not have been possible. Also a shout-out to all the friendly family ghosts who kept appearing and demanding, "Tell my story."

This is Ann Locasio's first book. After spending the first years of her life in Wales, Germany, England and Brazil, she attended three different high schools in the United States. She graduated from Cleveland State University in Cleveland, Ohio with a BA in Journalism. She has a Master of Divinity degree from Southern Methodist University and a PhD in Educational Psychology from the University of Texas at Austin. After being a pastor of United Methodist churches in Medina, Center Point, San Marcos, Goliad, and Lockhart, Texas, she now works as a certified peer support specialist at Austin State Hospital. She lives in Austin, Texas.